HBR'S 10 MUST READS

The definitive
management ideas
of the year from
Harvard Business Review.

2025

HBR's 10 Must Reads series is the definitive collection of ideas and best practices for aspiring and experienced leaders alike. These books offer essential reading selected from the pages of *Harvard Business Review* on topics critical to the success of every manager.

Titles include:

HBR's 10 Must Reads 2015
HBR's 10 Must Reads 2016
HBR's 10 Must Reads 2017
HBR's 10 Must Reads 2018
HBR's 10 Must Reads 2019
HBR's 10 Must Reads 2020
HBR's 10 Must Reads 2021
HBR's 10 Must Reads 2022
HBR's 10 Must Reads 2023
HBR's 10 Must Reads 2024
HBR's 10 Must Reads 2025
HBR's 10 Must Reads for Business Students
HBR's 10 Must Reads for CEOs
HBR's 10 Must Reads for Executive Teams
HBR's 10 Must Reads for Mid-Level Managers
HBR's 10 Must Reads for New Managers
HBR's 10 Must Reads on AI
HBR's 10 Must Reads on AI, Analytics, and the New Machine Age
HBR's 10 Must Reads on Boards
HBR's 10 Must Reads on Building a Great Culture
HBR's 10 Must Reads on Business Model Innovation
HBR's 10 Must Reads on Career Resilience
HBR's 10 Must Reads on Change Management (Volumes 1 and 2)
HBR's 10 Must Reads on Collaboration
HBR's 10 Must Reads on Communication (Volumes 1 and 2)
HBR's 10 Must Reads on Creativity
HBR's 10 Must Reads on Design Thinking
HBR's 10 Must Reads on Diversity

The definitive
management ideas
of the year from
Harvard Business Review.

2025

HARVARD BUSINESS REVIEW PRESS
Boston, Massachusetts

Library of Congress Cataloging-in-Publication Data

Names: Harvard Business Review Press, editor.
Title: HBR's 10 must reads 2025.
Other titles: HBR's 10 must reads (2025) | Harvard Business Review's ten
    must reads 2025
Description: Boston, Massachusetts : Harvard Business Review Press, [2024] |
    Series: HBR's 10 must reads | Includes bibliographical references and index.
Identifiers: LCCN 2024016870 (print) | LCCN 2024016871 (ebook) |
    ISBN 9798892790031 (paperback) | ISBN 9798892790048 (epub)
Subjects: LCSH: Management.
Classification: LCC HD31.2 .H369 2024 (print) | LCC HD31.2 (ebook) |
    DDC 658—dc23/eng/20240604
LC record available at https://lccn.loc.gov/2024016870
LC ebook record available at https://lccn.loc.gov/2024016871

ISBN: 979-8-89279-003-1
eISBN: 979-8-89279-004-8

Contents

Our mission at HBR is to help leaders move forward, and we try to distill that goal into the handful of must-read articles we select for each annual collection. When HBR editors come together to curate this list, it always begins as a medley. The articles we consider are as diverse as the leaders and organizations we serve: They might be big-picture pieces on building your next strategy; practical tips for coaching a struggling employee; or smart advice for thinking about your next career move. This year, shocks, crises, and how to react to them no longer dominate article headlines. Instead, questions focusing on the long term come to the fore: What do you want your workforce of the future to look like, and how can you make that vision a reality? How can you reshape your organization so that your people are free to innovate and are ready for a world of constant change? How will AI affect what you do in the next year, in five years, and beyond? The authors featured in *HBR's 10 Must Reads 2025* aren't just explaining the past and managing the present—they're looking ahead and preparing for what's coming next. This book will give you time and space to do the same. Take a moment to start imagining your future as a leader—both in your current organization and as you progress in your career.

We begin by taking on the topic at the top of all our minds: AI. As the pace of technological change continues to increase, millions of workers may need to be not just upskilled but *re*skilled—a complex societal challenge that may require them to change occupations entirely. So far, few companies have addressed their critical role in meeting this challenge. In **"Reskilling in the Age of AI,"** five authors—members of a collaboration between the Digital Data Design Institute at Harvard's Digital Reskilling Lab and the Boston Consulting Group's Henderson Institute—interviewed leaders at organizations around the world that are investing in large-scale reskilling programs. They found surprising evidence that employees *want* to reskill and that it's not just the responsibility of HR to get them there: It will take the work of every leader and manager, regardless of function.

Any future planning must consider growth. But with rising profit a nearly universal goal for leaders, HBS professor Gary P. Pisano identifies a question we usually fail to ask: **"How Fast Should Your Company Really Grow?"** If you go too fast, you may find yourself in a vicious cycle of stopgap measures and rapid hiring. And if they're not managed, these "growing pains" can become permanent. To expand consistently and at the right pace, you will need a strategy that encompasses three related decisions: how fast to grow, where to seek new sources of demand, and how to develop the financial, human, and organizational resources required. This article offers a framework for examining the critical interdependencies and trade-offs of those decisions in the context of a company's overall business strategy, its capabilities and culture, and external market dynamics.

How can you protect your energy and well-being amid the increasing and complex demands you face as a leader? Empathic leadership is vital in today's working world, but it's emotionally and physically exhausting. "I feel like I'm never enough," one *Fortune* 100 executive has lamented, "even in my empathy for my people. Anything going wrong with them means I've failed." The answer to this quandary lies in **"How to Sustain Your Empathy in Difficult Times,"** by the Stanford psychologist and neuroscientist Jamil Zaki. He outlines three steps: Start by caring for yourself; learn the difference between emotional empathy and empathic concern; and understand that empathy is a skill rather than a trait.

There's a huge, capable, and diverse talent pool out there that leaders aren't paying enough attention to: workers without college degrees. In **"The New-Collar Workforce,"** HBS professors Colleen Ammerman and Boris Groysberg, with Ginni Rometty, former CEO of IBM, demonstrate how to take a "skills first" approach to hiring and managing. It involves writing job descriptions that emphasize capabilities, not credentials; creating apprenticeships, internships, and training programs for people without college degrees; collaborating with educational institutions and other outside partners to expand the talent pool; helping hiring managers embrace skills-first thinking; bringing on board a critical mass of workers without degrees; and building a supportive organizational culture. A few companies are already taking this approach—and demonstrating its benefits for firms, workers, and society as a whole.

Robert I. Sutton and Huggy Rao of Stanford devoted eight years to learning about how leaders serve as trustees of others' time—how they prevent or remove barriers that undermine the zeal, damage the health, and throttle the creativity and productivity of good people. In **"Rid Your Organization of Obstacles That Infuriate Everyone,"** they focus on *addition sickness*: the unnecessary rules, procedures, communications, tools, and roles that seem to grow inexorably, stifling productivity and creativity. They show why companies are prone to this affliction and describe how leaders can treat it. The first step is to conduct a *good-riddance review* to identify obstacles that can and should be removed. The next is to employ *subtraction tools*—such as "the rule of halves" and "the subtraction game"—to eliminate those obstacles or make it difficult for people to add them in the first place.

Amid economic uncertainty, corporate belt-tightening, and efforts to dismantle diversity, equity, and inclusion efforts through both court rulings and legislation, the push for DEI has slowed. Much of the progress we've made over the past few years is at risk, and advocates for DEI may feel at a loss. Laura Morgan Roberts of the University of Virginia argues that to bring advocates and critics of diversity together, leaders must orient around a broader goal: creating the conditions in which *all* workers can flourish. In **"Where Does DEI Go from Here?"** you will learn to foster four freedoms at work: the freedom to be, the freedom to become, the freedom to fade (that is, to occasionally step back from performance pressure), and the freedom to fail. Interventions such as encouraging individual allyship, implementing strengths-based development programs, and enabling flexible work can make organizations safer and more welcoming for everyone.

Professional services partners are responsible not just for delivering services but also for the entire business-development process. As "rainmakers," they must build awareness of their expertise in the market to generate demand, identify and close new client business, deliver the work to the client, and renew and expand the relationship over time. But the old rainmaker playbook is out of date: Clients are much less loyal to firms and partners than they once were. In **"What Today's Rainmakers Do Differently,"** authors from the professional services consultancy DCM Insights lay out the key behaviors of *Activators*—their name for partners with the most successful approach. Activators connect networks of colleagues and clients, create value through collaboration, and commit to a proactive and consistent business-development routine. This article provides tips to help you identify Activators and build a team of them in your organization.

Governments around the world are increasingly intervening in the private sector through policies designed to help targeted domestic industries, such as automaking, energy, and semiconductor manufacturing. Those affected can expect to experience dramatic changes in their operating environments, such as new costs, investments to build manufacturing capacity, or incentives to trade with preferred partners. In **"The New Era of Industrial Policy Is Here,"** HBS professor Willy C. Shih outlines some of these policy approaches and offers a framework for responding to them. Leaders will need to understand the competing interests shaping the policies, engage and educate political leaders and their staffs, collaborate with upstream and downstream partners, and weigh the pros and cons of accepting government incentives. Corporate strategies created during what we will probably look back on as a "golden age of globalization" will have to be recast for a more fragmented world, taking into account varying country contexts and constraints and tailoring approaches to fit different markets.

When someone decides to buy an electric car, is it to prevent climate change? Of course not, say Frédéric Dalsace and Goutam Challagalla of IMD: "People buy cars because they need transportation; reducing their carbon footprint is an ancillary benefit." This example highlights something marketers often overlook when they are touting environmental or social benefits: Sustainable features have less impact on customers' decisions than basic product attributes do. **"How to Market Sustainable Products"** presents a new framework to help you deal with this challenge. It's critical to understand that some customers place a premium on sustainability, some value it only moderately, and some don't care about it and may even view it skeptically. You need a different approach for each of these types, and you can't ignore whether sustainable features enhance or diminish a product's basic features. Over time, winning companies will offer products that provide higher performance, environmental protection, *and* social well-being.

Business leaders are being urged to adopt a multistakeholder approach to governance in place of the shareholder-centered approach that has guided their work for several decades. But HBS professor Lynn S. Paine has found wide differences in how leaders understand stakeholder capitalism. That lack of clarity can put boards and executives on a collision course. **"What Does 'Stakeholder Capitalism' Mean to You?"** illuminates four versions of stakeholder capitalism that reflect significantly different levels of commitment and rest on very different rationales. *Instrumental*: Managers should respect stakeholders' interests when doing so will maximize long-term returns to shareholders. *Classic*: Companies have ethical and legal obligations to stakeholders that must be respected whether or not doing so is likely to maximize shareholder value. *Beneficial*: The corporate objective is to improve all stakeholders' well-being. And *structural*: To protect their interests, stakeholders other than shareholders should have formal powers in corporate governance. With these understandings in place, leaders can avoid fueling cynicism, alienation, and distrust—the opposite of what most proponents of stakeholder capitalism intend.

Our final article this year focuses on your own future and growth—no matter where you are in your career. Every HBR reader knows that running a business without a strategy is a losing proposition. But in our own lives, when faced with decisions both big and small, we often rely on emotion or intuition to guide us. A team of three BCG strategy consultants explain an alternative in **"Use Strategic Thinking to Create the Life You Want."** They suggest that you look at your current "portfolio"—the areas in which you spend your time and energy—to see whether you're investing the best of yourself in the right activities for your goals. Then you can identify where you need to make changes and ensure that you follow through with objectives and key results. With a little effort, you can develop a personal life strategy and summarize it on a single page. We have included a QR code in the chapter that will lead you to a helpful downloadable worksheet.

A new workforce. New needs for skills. New asks of managers. New industrial policy. And a new relationship with growth—both at work and in your own life. Read on, and keep looking toward the future as you move forward as a leader this year.

—The Editors

HBR'S 10 MUST READS

The definitive
management ideas
of the year from
Harvard Business Review.

2025

Reskilling in the Age of AI

by Jorge Tamayo, Leila Doumi, Sagar Goel, Orsolya Kovács-Ondrejkovic, and Raffaella Sadun

BACK IN 2019 the Organisation for Economic Co-operation and Development made a bold forecast. Within 15 to 20 years, it predicted, new automation technologies were likely to eliminate 14% of the world's jobs and radically transform another 32%. Those were sobering numbers, involving more than 1 billion people globally—and they didn't even factor in ChatGPT and the new wave of generative AI that has recently taken the market by storm.

Today advances in technology are changing the demand for skills at an accelerated pace. New technologies can not only handle a growing number of repetitive and manual tasks but also perform increasingly sophisticated kinds of knowledge-based work—such as research, coding, and writing—that have long been considered safe from disruption. The average half-life of skills is now less than five years, and in some tech fields it's as low as two and a half years. Not all knowledge workers will lose their jobs in the years ahead, of course, but as they carry out their daily tasks, many of them may well discover that AI and other new technologies have so significantly altered the nature of what they do that in effect they're working in completely new fields.

To cope with these disruptions, a number of organizations are already investing heavily in upskilling their workforces. One recent BCG study suggests that such investments represent as much as 1.5%

of those organizations' total budgets. But upskilling alone won't be enough. If the OECD estimates are correct, in the coming decades millions of workers may need to be entirely *reskilled*—a fundamental and profoundly complex societal challenge that will require workers not only to acquire new skills but to use them to change occupations.

Companies have a critical role to play in addressing this challenge, and it's in their best interests to get going on it in a serious way right now. Among those that have embraced the reskilling challenge, only a handful have done so effectively, and even *their* efforts have often been subscale and of limited impact, which leads to a question: Now that the need for a reskilling revolution is apparent, what must companies do to make it happen?

In our work at the HBS Digital Reskilling Lab and the BCG Henderson Institute we have been studying this question in depth, and as part of that effort we interviewed leaders at almost 40 organizations around the world that are investing in large-scale reskilling programs. During those interviews we discussed common challenges, heard stories of early success, and discovered that many of those companies are thinking in important new ways about why, when, and how to reskill. In synthesizing what we've learned, we've become aware of five paradigm shifts that are emerging in reskilling—shifts that companies will need to understand and embrace if they hope to succeed in adapting dynamically to the rapidly evolving era of automation and AI.

In this article we'll explore those shifts. We'll show how some companies are implementing them, and we'll review the unexpected challenges they've encountered and the promising wins they've achieved.

1. Reskilling Is a Strategic Imperative

During times of disruption, when many jobs are threatened, companies have often turned to reskilling to soften the blow of layoffs, assuage feelings of guilt about social responsibility, and create a positive PR narrative. But most of the companies we spoke with have moved beyond that narrow approach and now recognize reskilling

Idea in Brief

The Situation

New technologies can not only handle a growing number of repetitive and manual tasks but also perform sophisticated kinds of knowledge-based work—such as research, coding, and writing—that have long been considered safe from disruption.

The Challenge

To cope, many organizations are investing heavily in upskilling their workforces, but those efforts alone won't be enough. In the coming decades millions of workers may need to be entirely reskilled—a profoundly complex societal challenge.

The Path Forward

Some companies have recently launched successful reskilling efforts. Five important paradigm shifts have emerged from their efforts that other companies will need to embrace if they hope to adapt to the new era of automation and AI.

as a strategic imperative. That shift reflects profound changes in the labor market, which is increasingly constrained by the aging of the working population, the emergence of new occupations, and an increasing need for employees to develop skills that are company-specific. Against this backdrop effective reskilling initiatives are critical, because they allow companies to build competitive advantage quickly by developing talent that is not readily available in the market and filling skills gaps that are instrumental to achieving their strategic objectives—before and better than their competitors do.

In recent years several major companies have embraced this approach. Infosys, for example, has reskilled more than 2,000 cybersecurity experts with various adjacent competencies and capability levels. Vodafone aims to draw from internal talent to fill 40% of its software developer needs. And Amazon, through its Machine Learning University, has enabled thousands of employees who initially had little experience in machine learning to become experts in the field.

Some companies now consider reskilling a core part of their employee value proposition and a strategic means of balancing workforce supply and demand. At those companies employees are encouraged to reskill for roles that appeal to them. Mahindra & Mahindra,

Wipro, and Ericsson have policies, tools, and IT platforms that promote reskilling resources and available jobs—as does McDonald's, where restaurant employees have access to an app called Archways to Opportunity that maps skills learned on the job to career paths within the company and in other industries.

Finally, some companies are using reskilling to tap into broader talent pools and attract candidates who wouldn't otherwise be considered for open positions. ICICI Bank—headquartered in Mumbai and employing more than 130,000 people—runs an intense, academy-like reskilling program that prepares graduates, often from diverse backgrounds, for frontline managerial jobs. The program reskills some 2,500 to 4,000 employees each year. CVS used a similar approach during the Covid-19 pandemic to hire, train, and onboard people (some of them laid-off hospitality workers) to create capacity for its critical vaccine and testing services.

2. Reskilling Is the Responsibility of Every Leader and Manager

Traditionally, reskilling is considered part of the overall corporate-learning function. When that's the case, responsibility for the design and implementation of the program is often siloed within HR, and its failure or success is measured very narrowly—in terms of the number of trainings delivered, the cost per learner, and similar training-specific metrics. According to a recent BCG report, only 24% of polled companies make a clear connection between corporate strategy and reskilling efforts. Reskilling investments need a profound commitment from HR leaders, of course, but unless the rest of the organization understands the strategic relevance of those investments, it's very hard to obtain the relentless and distributed effort that such initiatives require to succeed.

At most of the organizations where we interviewed, reskilling initiatives are visibly championed by senior leaders, often CEOs and chief operating officers. They work hard to articulate for the rest of the company the connection between reskilling and strategy and to ensure that leadership and management teams understand their shared responsibility for implementing these programs. For example, as part of its ongoing digital transformation, Ericsson has developed a multiyear strategy devoted to upskilling and reskilling. The effort involves systematically defining critical skills connected to strategy, which correspond to a variety of accelerator programs, skill journeys, and skill-shifting targets—most of them dedicated to transforming telecommunications experts into AI and data-science experts. The company considers this a high-priority, high-investment project and has made it part of the objectives and key results that executives review quarterly. In just three years Ericsson has upskilled more than 15,000 employees in AI and automation.

Similarly, the executive team at CVS has made training and reskilling an integral part of the company's business strategies. Each individual business leader is now responsible for designing and delivering workforce-reskilling plans to help the company reach its goals, and the ability to do so is factored in to performance assessments. Amazon, too, has famously committed to reskilling as a core strategic objective and now mentions it prominently in its leadership manifesto for managers. The visibility of this commitment contributes to Amazon's ability to achieve scale in reskilling programs.

3. Reskilling Is a Change-Management Initiative

To design and implement ambitious reskilling programs, companies must do a lot more than just train employees: They must create an organizational context conducive to success. To do that they need to ensure the right mindset and behaviors among employees and managers alike. From this perspective, reskilling is akin to a change-management initiative, because it requires a focus on many different tasks simultaneously.

Let's consider several of the most important.

Understanding supply and demand

To create a successful reskilling program, companies need a sophisticated understanding of supply (skills available internally and externally) and demand (skills needed to beat the competition).

A useful way to develop this understanding is with a "skill taxonomy"—a detailed description of the capabilities needed for each occupation at a company. Employers used to put a lot of effort into creating such taxonomies from scratch, but many leading companies now rely on external providers for the bulk of the work. HSBC, for example, has adopted the taxonomy published by the World Economic Forum and customized it slightly to add skills specific to parts of its business. Similarly, SAP, which used to maintain an in-house taxonomy of 7,000 skills, has recently started working with Lightcast, which keeps a continually updated skill database. But developing a skill taxonomy is only the first step. Next comes the difficult job of deciding which skills get mapped to which jobs. Managers from different divisions may disagree about this. Such disagreement is often symptomatic of a deeper misalignment, and companies will need to resolve that before they undertake any major reskilling initiative.

Leaders must also determine what skills they will need in the future—a dynamic process that's critical for strategic reskilling programs. To do that well, they should focus on figuring out what skills the current strategy demands. Here they'll need to develop a rigorous strategic workforce-planning methodology. The European insurance company Allianz has done interesting work on this front: It regularly translates forecasted business growth into talent demand, focusing on the number of people needed in various jobs and the skills they'll require. The model, which is updated as part of the annual planning process, involves economic scenario planning and takes into account the possible effects of digitalization on the workforce.

Recruiting and evaluating

Traditionally, candidates are recruited for training opportunities or internal roles on the basis of their degrees or relevant work experience, but that obviously doesn't work for reskilled workers. A well-developed skill taxonomy can help here, by allowing organizations to think about enrollment policies in light of skill adjacencies, which can facilitate the transition from one skill set to another. Novartis has implemented an AI-powered internal talent marketplace that predicts, matches, and offers roles and projects related to employees' skills and goals. In our research we've also found that if reskilling programs are to succeed, companies must develop a clear set of enrollment criteria for employees, not all of whom will have the right combination of motivation and personality traits to be a good fit for reskilling.

Shaping the mindset of middle managers

Middle managers are often resistant to the idea of reskilling, for two main reasons: They worry (1) that their reports won't be able to keep up with their regular responsibilities while being reskilled, and (2) that once their reports *are* reskilled, they'll move to other parts of the organization. In both cases this can lead to "talent hoarding," in which managers try to hold on to their favorite reports by denying them the ability to participate in reskilling. Several of the companies we spoke with have addressed this problem by making talent development an explicit managerial responsibility. Wipro evaluates managers according to their teams' participation in training offers, and Amazon promotes leaders on the basis of a performance assessment that includes the question "How have you developed your team?" Middle managers may also resist the idea of hiring reskilled employees, believing that they're not as desirable as traditionally skilled workers. This problem can be addressed by involving managers in the design and delivery of reskilling programs and by providing sensitivity and unconscious-bias training. No matter what form the resistance takes, senior leaders' role modeling in support of reskilling is vital to overcoming it.

Building skills in the flow of work

It can be costly and logistically challenging to take employees away from their day jobs to participate in training. And adults tend not to like or learn well in classroom-style situations. In a 2021 BCG survey 65% of the 209,000 participating workers said they prefer to learn on the job. As a result, the best approach for reskilling is to do as much training as possible by means of shadowing assignments, internal apprenticeships, and trial periods. The reskilling program at ICICI Bank, for example, consists of a four-month vocational residency, during which employees take part in simulation-style trainings for the managerial role they hope to get, and an eight-month deployment in the field that involves a structured internship in a bank branch and closely shadowing a current manager.

Matching and integrating reskilled employees

Employees need to be matched with new jobs. Our interview data shows that if destination roles are clearly described in advance, employees become more interested in reskilling because new career trajectories become apparent to them, and the reskilling itself becomes more effective because it's more position-specific. Once in their new jobs, reskilled employees need several kinds of support to integrate successfully: help with learning new work norms and culture, building networks, and developing soft skills. Here coaching and mentoring can be particularly effective tools. Amazon has demonstrated leadership in this area: It runs a variety of mentoring programs for reskilled employees, among them a buddy system, part of its Grow Our Own Talent program, that connects previous and current program participants. The company also provides career coaching for employees who are making particularly difficult transitions, such as from warehouse worker to software developer.

4. Employees *Want* to Reskill—When It Makes Sense

Many of the companies we spoke with mentioned that one of their biggest challenges was simply persuading employees to embark on reskilling programs. That's understandable: Reskilling requires a lot of effort and can set a major life change in motion, and the outcome isn't guaranteed. The OECD reports that only a very small fraction of workers typically take part in standard training programs, and those who do are often the ones who need them the least.

But workers may be more willing to engage in reskilling than prior data suggests. BCG data shows, for example, that 68% of workers are aware of coming disruptions in their fields and are willing to reskill to remain competitively employed. The key to success in this domain, our interviews suggest, is to treat workers respectfully and make the benefits of their participation in reskilling initiatives clear. As one of our interviewees explains, "The secret to scaling up reskilling programs is to design a product your employees actually like." So how can organizations do that? We have several suggestions.

Treat employees as partners

Because reskilling programs are often associated with organizational disruption and job loss—or at least job change—leaders often avoid talking openly about the rationale for the programs and the opportunities they present. But employees are more likely to participate if they understand why the programs are being implemented and have had a role in creating them. Aware of this, several of the companies we spoke with made a point of being honest and clear about why they were creating reskilling programs and involving workers early. One large auto manufacturer, for example, told its diesel engineers that because of changes in the automobile industry, it had less and less need for their skills; it presented its program as a way of ensuring that they would have new jobs and job security in the years ahead. The companies also told us that in designing and implementing reskilling programs, it's critical to align with worker councils and unions early on and to involve them in advocating for the programs.

Design programs from the employee point of view

Reskilling programs require participants to make a major investment of time. So it's important to try to reduce the risk, cost, and effort involved and to provide (almost) guaranteed outcomes. Amazon allows employees in its Career Choice program to pursue everything from bachelor's degrees to certificates—and covers all costs in advance. That has proved to be a key factor in scaling up the program, which has already had more than 130,000 participants. CVS, for its part, uses an effective "train in place" model for new employees.

Dedicate adequate time and attention to the task

Because reskilling involves occupational change, it usually requires intensive learning, which is possible only if employees have the time and mental space they need to succeed. To that end, four times a year Vodafone dedicates days during which employees may devote themselves entirely to learning and personal development. Bosch goes even further: To help traditional engineers at the company earn degrees and get training in emerging fields, its Mission to Move program covers the cost of tuition and time spent learning for as much as two days a week for a whole year. It even gives participants days off before exams to prepare.

Naturally, providing employees the time and space for skilling can be harder in industries where most workers are hourly or shift-based. Iberdrola, a renewable energy company, faced this challenge as it digitized. Because it was embracing new technologies, the company realized it would need to reskill 3,300 employees in various hourly roles. Its leaders got the job done by working closely with frontline managers to ensure that operations weren't disrupted by workers taking time off for training. The company considered all training hours to be work hours and paid employees for them accordingly.

5. Reskilling Takes a Village

Companies have tended to think of reskilling as an organization-level challenge, believing that they have to do the job by and for themselves. But many of the companies where we interviewed have recognized that reskilling takes place in an ecosystem in which a number of actors have roles to play. Governments can incentivize reskilling investments by means of funds, policies, and public programs; industry can team up with academia to develop new skill-building techniques; and NGOs can play a role in connecting corporate talent needs with disadvantaged and marginalized talent groups. Coalitions of companies may be more effective at the reskilling challenge than single organizations are.

When designing reskilling programs for the rapidly evolving era of AI and automation, companies need to harness the potential of this wider ecosystem. We've identified several ways in which they can do so.

Consider industry partnerships

Instead of thinking of themselves as competitors for a limited talent pool, companies can team up to conduct joint training efforts, which may significantly attenuate some of the challenges outlined above. For example, industrywide skill taxonomies would provide a useful infrastructure and could in some cases help companies pool the knowledge and resources needed to invest in certain types of capabilities, such as cutting-edge AI skills, which are so new that individual organizations may not yet have the knowledge or the capacity to develop solutions on their own. Industry coalitions could also reassure participants that their investments in learning might open up broader future opportunities.

The Technology in Finance Immersion Programme, offered by the Institute of Banking and Finance Singapore, a nonprofit industry association, is a case in point. The program aims to build up an industry pipeline of capabilities in key technology areas, with participation from all major banks, insurance players, and asset managers in the country, to meet the talent needs of the financial services sector. Similarly, within the European Union a variety of stakeholders have formed the Automotive Skills Alliance, which is dedicated to the "re-skilling and up-skilling of workers in the automotive sector."

Partner with nonprofits to reach diverse talent

Many reskilling nonprofits work with populations that are underrepresented in the workforce. By teaming up with these nonprofits, companies can significantly expand access to talent and employment opportunities in ways that benefit both parties, often at low cost. Some of the ongoing reskilling efforts we learned of in our research involve corporate partnerships with such innovative entities as OneTen (which helps Black workers in the United States), Year Up (which helps disadvantaged youths in the United States), Joblinge (which helps disadvantaged youths in Germany), and RISE 2.0 (a BCG program that helps workers in Singapore without a digital background move into digital roles). Year Up stands out among these initiatives for its careful use of statistical techniques to study the impact of its training on participants. Since 2011 the program has placed more than 40,000 young people in corporate roles and internships that would have been inaccessible to them without the reskilling support and network it provided. The program has an 80% placement rate at more than 250 participating companies.

Partner with local colleges and training providers
Companies have a lot to gain by teaming up with educational institutions in their reskilling efforts. Examples of such partnerships include the UK-government-funded Institutes of Technology, which bring together colleges and major employers to provide practical technical training for workers without tech backgrounds, in ways that allow companies to quickly react to new technologies and meet rapidly evolving skills needs; and BMW's collaboration with the German Federal Employment Agency and the Association of German Chambers of Industry and Commerce, which supports the transition to electric vehicles with reskilling programs aimed at industrial electricians.

———————

Many companies have an intuitive understanding of the need to embrace the reskilling paradigm shifts discussed in this article, and some, admirably, have already made tremendous commitments to doing so. But their efforts are hampered by two important limitations: a lack of rigor when it comes to the measurement and evaluation of what actually works, and a lack of information about how to generalize and scale up the demonstrably successful features of reskilling programs. To adapt in the years ahead to the rapidly accelerating pace of technological change, companies will have to develop ways to learn—in a systematic, rigorous, experimental, and long-term way—from the many reskilling investments that are being made today. Only then will the reskilling revolution really take off.

Originally published in September–October 2023. Reprint R2306C

How Fast Should Your Company Really Grow?

by Gary P. Pisano

PERHAPS NO ISSUE attracts more senior leadership attention than growth does. And for good reason. Growth—in revenues and profits—is the yardstick by which we tend to measure the competitive fitness and health of companies and determine the quality and compensation of its management. Analysts, investors, and boards pepper CEOs about growth prospects to get insight into stock prices. Employees are attracted to faster-growing companies because they offer better opportunities for advancement, higher pay, and greater job security. Suppliers prefer faster-growing customers because working with them improves their own growth prospects. Given the choice, most companies and their stakeholders would choose faster growth over slower growth.

While sustained profitable growth is a nearly universal goal, it is an elusive one for many companies. Empirical research that I and others have conducted on the long-term patterns of growth in U.S. corporations suggests that when inflation is taken into account, most companies barely grow. For instance, in an analysis of 10,897 publicly held U.S. companies from 1976 to 2019, my research associate Catherine Piner and I found that firms in the top quartile grew at an inflation-adjusted average of 11.8% per year, but those in the lower three quartiles experienced little or no growth (0.3%,

0.03%, and -0.5%, respectively). And the majority of firms in the top quartile were unable to sustain superior growth performance for more than a few years. Although challenging to achieve, sustained profitable growth is not impossible, however. In our analysis, we found that only about 15% of the companies in the top growth quartile in 1985 were able to sustain their top-quartile performance for at least 30 years.

Over the past two decades, I have tried to understand why some companies are more effective at sustaining growth and what senior leaders can do to navigate the organizational challenges it poses. In addition to quantitative statistical analysis of large samples of U.S. companies over multiple decades, I have conducted case studies of more than 20 companies in a variety of industries, including semiconductors, software, health care, life sciences, restaurants, airlines, alcoholic beverages, luxury goods, apparel, hotels, and automobiles. I've also gleaned additional insights from my experience consulting for (and serving on the boards of) companies ranging in size from startups to some of the world's largest corporations.

I have found that while the usual explanations for slow or minimal growth—market forces and technological changes such as disruptive innovation—play a role, many companies' growth problems are self-inflicted. Specifically, firms approach growth in a highly reactive, opportunistic manner. When market demand is booming, they go on hiring binges, throw resources at developing new capacity, and build out organizational infrastructure without thinking through the implications—for example, whether their operating systems and processes can scale, how rapid growth might affect corporate culture, whether they can attract the human capital necessary to deliver that growth, and what would happen if demand slows. In the process of chasing growth, companies can easily destroy the things that made them successful in the first place, such as their capacity for innovation, their agility, their great customer service, or their unique cultures. When demand slows, pressures to maintain historical growth rates can lead to quick-fix solutions such as costly acquisitions or drastic cuts in R&D, other capabilities, and training. The damage caused by these moves only exacerbates the growth problems.

Idea in Brief

The Problem

Sustained profitable growth is a nearly universal corporate goal, but it is an elusive one. Empirical research suggests that when inflation is taken into account, most companies barely grow at all.

The Cause

While external factors play a role, most companies' growth problems are self-inflicted: Too many firms approach growth in a highly reactive, opportunistic manner.

The Solution

To grow profitably over the long term, companies need a strategy that addresses three key decisions: how fast to grow (rate of growth); where to seek new sources of demand (direction of growth); and how to amass the resources needed to grow (method of growth).

Sustaining profitable growth requires a delicate balance between the pursuit of market opportunities (demand) and the creation of the capabilities and capacity needed to exploit those opportunities (supply). To proactively manage that balance, companies need a growth strategy that explicitly addresses three interrelated decisions: how fast to grow (the target rate of growth); where to seek new sources of demand (the direction of growth); and how to amass the financial, human, and organizational resources needed to grow (the method of growth).

Each of those decisions involves trade-offs that must be considered in concert with a company's overall business strategy, its capabilities and culture, and external market dynamics. (See the sidebar "The Perils of an Unintegrated Growth Strategy.") My rate-direction-method (RDM) framework highlights the critical interdependencies between decisions that are all too often made separately. Using the framework to illuminate the trade-offs, companies can create a balanced growth strategy.

Rate: What Is the Right Pace of Growth?

The answer to this question seems obvious: as fast as possible. But taking a strategic perspective means that companies choose a target growth rate that reflects their capacity to effectively exploit

The Perils of an Unintegrated Growth Strategy

B.GOOD, A QUICK-SERVE RESTAURANT founded in 2004, offers a cautionary tale about the need to make rate, direction, and method choices in an integrated manner when crafting a growth strategy. As a case study by Francesca Gino, Paul Green Jr., and Bradley Staats reveals, B.good has an innovative value proposition: Unlike most companies in the industry, B.good makes its burgers and other fast-food offerings using fresh, local ingredients. In addition, it cultivates a "family" culture for employees and customers: The founders got to know many employees and often reached out to them on special occasions or in difficult circumstances. Frontline employees were encouraged to greet customers by name and recommend members of their own families for jobs at the company.

B.good's value proposition and its focus on culture created challenges operationally and organizationally. The focus on "fresh and local" and the unique cultural model made franchising—which requires more standardization and less corporate control over human resource decisions—and geographic expansion more difficult.

For the first eight years of B.good's existence, it pursued a growth strategy compatible with its constraints: It opened only eight restaurants, all in the immediate Boston area and all completely company-owned. It had a cohesive growth strategy aligned with its core value proposition.

opportunities. Growth is a strategic choice with implications for a company's operating processes, financing, human resource strategy, organizational design, business model, and culture.

In finance, the concept of a sustainable growth rate is well understood: It is the fastest a company can grow without having to sell equity or borrow. But talent, organizational know-how, operational capabilities, management systems, and even culture are also resources required to produce goods and services, and they, too, can become bottlenecks constraining growth. A competent CFO will keep a company from growing faster than its financial resources will allow. Unfortunately, CEOs and leaders of other functions often do not apply the same disciplined thinking to nonfinancial resources (which constitute the vast majority of a firm's value). For example, rapidly growing

But then the company changed its growth strategy. It began to add outlets very quickly, a rate decision. By 2019, it operated 69 stores across the Northeast, South, Midwest, and Canada—a direction decision. And to finance growth, it began to sell franchises, a method choice; by 2019, 20% of its outlets were franchised.

In the aftermath of this change in strategy, the company struggled. Every time it expanded into a new geography, it needed to develop a new supplier base to fulfill its fresh and local promise. And every franchise selection required a time-consuming process to make sure the franchisee shared the founders' philosophy. The company's leaders should have realized that they faced a strategic choice: Either align its growth strategy with its core value proposition—which would have meant slower growth, less aggressive geographic expansion, and less franchising—or change its value proposition and culture to enable faster growth, broader geographic expansion, and more franchising. They tried to have it both ways, and it didn't work. As of 2023, the company was down to just 13 outlets, 11 of which were in metropolitan Boston and one each in Maine and New Hampshire.

companies may downplay gaps between what their staffing levels, management capabilities, and operating processes can deliver and what is required to meet demand, seeing them as transitory "growing pains." This approach can trigger a vicious circle. Shortfalls in critical capabilities can lead to quality and other operating problems, which in turn become a drain on already-stretched resources. With no time to design and install systems adequate to handle the growth, companies often attempt to "catch up" through massive hiring and infrastructure spending and other stopgap measures. Worker burnout and attrition are not uncommon. These firms find themselves with a patchwork of suboptimal systems, an unwieldy infrastructure, an exhausted workforce, and a tarnished reputation in the market. And the so-called growing pains turn out to be not so temporary.

A case in point is Peloton. During the pandemic, it reacted to the surge in demand for its exercise bikes and treadmills with a furious effort to expand manufacturing capacity and distribution. The expansion pushed the company's supply chain beyond its capabilities, which led to quality and customer service problems (including two recalls). The cooling of pandemic-fueled demand left the company with a bloated cost structure.

The right strategy for many firms may be saying no to faster growth—even if the opportunities are tempting in the short term. Pal's Sudden Service, a quick-serve restaurant chain with 31 outlets in the southeastern United States that Francesca Gino, Bradley Staats, and I studied, is an example of a company that has taken an exceptionally disciplined approach to growth. Founded in 1956, Pal's has eschewed the rapid expansion of outlets favored by many fast-food chains. Since 1985, when it opened its third outlet, it has added, on average, less than one new restaurant per year and it has never opened more than one restaurant in any year. Pal's boasts one of the highest revenues per square foot in the industry: $2,500 versus $650 for the typical burger chain. In an industry where scale economies are critical, the chain's excellent financial performance is surprising. A key ingredient to its success is its operating system, which is designed around lean manufacturing principles. Every process, from where to place the ketchup on a burger to how far to open a hot dog bun, has been carefully studied and specified. The company's menu is limited to a few basic items such as hamburgers, hot dogs, sandwiches, fries, and milkshakes.

With such a profitable and rigorous operating model, and seemingly unlimited demand in the United States for its products, a massive and lucrative expansion would appear to make sense. Yet the chain's leadership recognizes that a unique aspect of its model places a limit on how fast it can grow: its obsession with quality. Pal's has an extremely low rate of order errors: one error per 3,600 orders versus one error per 15 orders for the industry. That level of quality not only allows Pal's to save costs on food waste, which is critical in an industry with low margins, but it also enables the company to have one of the fastest throughput times in the industry. In a drive-through operation, order errors cause delays for every customer down the line. Pal's is able to serve more customers at peak hours, and that translates directly into higher revenue.

But the emphasis on quality also requires significant investment in resources—in particular, for extensive training and building the right culture in the workforce. At Pal's, workers are trained for weeks on each process and must pass a certification test before they can make products for customers. They must be recertified periodically to ensure that their skills are up to par. All Pal's stores are managed by "owner-operators" (who are not actually owners but whose compensation is tied 100% to their individual store's profits). Pal's believes that these managers are critical to nurturing the culture of quality and to training and developing talent. All manager candidates are put through an extensive screening process, and selected candidates, regardless of their prior industry experience, attend the company's leadership-development program. It normally takes candidates three years to be allowed to run their own store. The company's growth strategy is dictated by the availability of store managers: When Pal's has a candidate ready, it will open a new store.

Notice the difference between the Pal's approach to growth and that of most other companies. Pal's does not set a growth goal on the basis of market potential or target financial returns. Instead, it recognizes its critical bottleneck resource—in this case, store managers—and paces growth according to the rate at which it can develop them. This approach has almost certainly meant slower growth in number of stores and revenue, but it has been critical to maintaining the company's unique operating model and its superior financial performance.

In my research, I've found that most companies think of growth potential in terms of "demand side" factors: external trends, market share, and other metrics such as total addressable market. These are important, of course, but they are only half the story. Supply-side constraints matter just as much: High demand potential does not translate into profitable growth unless an organization has or can develop the capabilities needed to meet that demand. So a strategic perspective on growth means analyzing the company's sustainable

Sustainable growth is elusive

To evaluate patterns of growth performance over time, we identified 680 companies for which we could calculate 10-year rolling average growth rates for at least 25 years during the period 1985 to 2019. In this sample, we identified the top quartile of growers in 1985 according to their previous 10-year rolling average and then examined the performance of those 170 firms over the subsequent 34 years. Not surprisingly, most fell out of the top quartile over time.

Of the original 170 companies, only seven (Walmart, UPS, Southwest, Publix, Johnson & Johnson, Danaher, and Berkshire Hathaway) appeared in the top quartile for all 34 years. Only 19 companies stayed in the top quartile for at least 30 years. Companies appeared in the top quartile for an average of 19 years. When we repeated this analysis using three different starting periods (1990, 1995, 2000), the general patterns were the same.

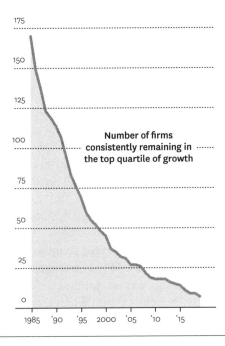

growth rate (considering all resources, not just money) and then thinking through the trade-offs inherent in faster or slower growth. For instance, there may be excellent strategic reasons to grow more quickly (for example, a market where first-mover advantages or network effects are present), but that faster growth must be weighed against the potential harm it creates.

Direction of Growth: Scale, Scope, or Diversify?

Since demand ultimately fuels growth, selecting which market opportunities to pursue is a critical component of a company's overall growth strategy. Some companies seek growth by scaling in their core market. Others broaden their scope into adjacent products and services. Still others diversify into a range of seemingly unrelated industries. Which strategies are most profitable over the long term has long been a topic of hot debate, and my research suggests there is no simple answer.

Let's return to the analysis of nearly 11,000 companies from 1976 to 2019. Among the fastest long-term growers, some companies—such as Walmart, UPS, Southwest Airlines, and Publix—grew by scaling in their core markets, replicating their model in new geographic markets, or adding ancillary services closely aligned with their core service operations. Others—such as Danaher, Johnson & Johnson (for which I have provided consulting services in the past), and Berkshire Hathaway—took the opposite approach in pursuing diversification strategies.

How should companies decide which path to take in their pursuit of growth? It is tempting to think about such choices as simply a matter of identifying and exploiting immature, unsaturated markets with rapid overall growth potential. While market dynamics matter, there are other factors to consider. For example, from 1980 to 2019 the average compound annual growth rate of the domestic U.S. travel market (in terms of "revenue passenger miles," or the number of miles traveled by paying passengers) was a modest 5.3%. Southwest Airlines, however, enjoyed a brisk average CAGR of 15.3%. It accomplished that by developing unique operating capabilities (such as fast turnaround of aircraft) that enabled it to efficiently provide point-to-point service on routes that traditional competitors either ignored or served only through inconvenient hub-and-spoke models.

I've found that even in higher-growth industries, the distribution of growth rates tends to be highly skewed, with a small set of firms accounting for the lion's share of industry growth. Consider the semiconductor industry. From 2015 to 2020, the top 10 semiconductor companies grew at an average annual compound rate of 9.2%. However, excluding the two fastest growers during this time (Nvidia, with a CAGR of 27%, and Taiwan Semiconductor, with a CAGR of 12.3%), the average dropped to 6.5%. Nvidia's rapid growth stems from its capabilities in the design of powerful graphics processing units, or GPUs. Those capabilities helped Nvidia capture a 61% market share in the fast-growing market for chips used to power machine-learning and other artificial intelligence applications; the next closest rival is Intel, with a 16% share. The AI chip market offers high growth potential only to companies with the R&D capabilities to compete there—for others, it is not a particularly attractive opportunity.

The basic question that companies must address is: In which markets do our capabilities and other unique resources (such as brand, customer relationships, reputation, and so on) provide us with a competitive advantage? A scale-focused strategy will tend to revolve around deep, market-specific capabilities. Think about pharmaceutical companies. The capabilities that enable them to grow are their scientific prowess in drug discovery, understanding of clinical development and regulatory approval processes, and access to payer networks. While incredibly valuable for scale-based growth in pharmaceutical products, none of those capabilities transfers readily to other industries (including medical devices and diagnostics, which have different regulatory paths and market-access dynamics).

Successful scope strategies, in contrast, require the development of broader, general-purpose capabilities and resources that can be leveraged across market segments and lines of business. In some industries, brand equity is the basis for scope expansion. Consider the potent role that brand has played in Nike's explosive growth over the past several decades as it expanded from being a maker of running shoes to a powerhouse across the sports apparel and equipment industry. In other cases, broad technological assets and capabilities open doors to new businesses. While conducting research on diversification patterns across more than 28,000 companies from 1975 to 2004, my colleague Dominika Randle and I analyzed patterns of patent citations to understand the degree to which a company's technological capabilities were broadly applicable across markets. Our analysis showed that the companies with the most general-purpose technological assets (those that could be applied across multiple industries) were the most likely to diversify.

Method of Growth: How to Grow?

All growth requires access to new resources: financial capital, people and talent, brand, distribution channels, and so on. But there are various ways companies can choose to obtain them. A classic choice leaders face is how much to focus on organic growth versus growth by acquisition. Companies must also make decisions about how to finance growth, whether to vertically integrate or outsource to or partner with other firms, and whether to franchise or build out company-owned operations.

Obtaining any growth-fueling resource—money, people, brand, access to capabilities, and so on—involves trade-offs. Building up resources organically can take time (and thus result in slower growth), but those internally developed resources can often be more precisely aligned and integrated with a company's unique value proposition. Partnering and outsourcing might provide a faster route to growth, especially for younger companies trying to bring products to market, but it can mean ceding control of activities critical to the value proposition.

Method decisions are tightly connected to choices about the rate and direction of growth. Consider the case of Virgin Group, which my colleague Elena Corsi and I studied. The company's growth strategy is to expand into new markets and industries where the Virgin brand can drive customer acquisition. The company's leaders consider the Virgin brand—along with fresh approaches to providing high-quality customer service—to be the firm's critical resource. In many ways, Virgin's rate of growth depends on the rate at which the brand can be monetized in new markets.

The privately owned Virgin Group has increasingly used licensing of its brand to drive growth. To raise the capital needed for acquisitions to enter new markets, Virgin divests existing businesses. In such cases, it generally strikes a licensing agreement with the acquirer for the right to use the Virgin brand. As a result of its aggressive use of licensing, Virgin Group's most valuable asset, the Virgin brand, is increasingly under the control of organizations of which it is not a majority owner and over which it can exercise only limited control. This creates risks to the brand, even with vigilant monitoring and strict contractual clauses. While disputes between Virgin and its licensees are rare, they have happened. Looking at Virgin's growth strategy through the rate-direction-method lens helps us understand the trade-offs the company has made. The licensing-driven method of growth enables broader diversification and faster growth, but it creates brand equity risks. A lower-risk approach would be to use less licensing (for instance, let the Virgin brand be used only in companies in which Virgin Group owns a majority share), but this would most likely mean less diversification and less growth.

What Makes a Great Growth Strategist

As companies grapple with the central question of how fast to grow, they'll need leaders who understand the key decisions to be made and their inherent trade-offs. Good growth strategists are keenly aware of the nonfinancial constraints—such as systems, processes, human capital, and culture—on their company's sustainable growth rate. They know that growing faster than capabilities dictate is possible in the short term but that doing so over the long term can cause lasting damage to reputation and culture. Good growth strategists do not fall into the trap of thinking they can grow fast now and fix things later. They recognize that more-measured growth over a sustained period will lead to much better financial results than explosive growth for a short period of time.

Great growth strategists, however, go beyond avoiding traps and accepting trade-offs. They proactively look for ways to augment the resources that constrain short-term growth and focus on the continuous accumulation of new resources and capabilities that open options for future growth, either through scaling in core markets or through entry into other markets. They see investments in training, processes, systems, technology, and culture as means to break growth bottlenecks and raise a company's sustainable growth rate. They are comfortable with leading organizational change. Finally, they are obsessed with human capital. They recognize that among the many resources shaping a company's growth potential, the quality, talent, and mindset of its people are the most important. Great growth strategists realize that sustained profitable growth is never going to be easy, but without the right human capital, it will be impossible.

Originally published in March–April 2024. Reprint R2402B

How to Sustain Your Empathy in Difficult Times

by Jamil Zaki

WHEN I STARTED STUDYING EMPATHY, nearly 20 years ago, its status in the workplace was controversial. Many people believed that empathic leadership—which draws on the ability to understand, care about, and vicariously experience the emotions of others—was too "soft" for the hard-charging, competitive world of business.

By now dozens of studies have demonstrated the opposite. Empathy is not a weakness but something of a workplace superpower. Employees are more satisfied in their jobs, more willing to take creative risks, and more likely to help their colleagues if they work in empathic organizations. They are far less likely to report severe burnout or to develop physical symptoms of stress, and are more resilient in the face of adversity. They also tend to stay: A 2022 Gallup survey of more than 15,000 U.S. employees found that those with caring employers were far less likely than others to actively search for a new job. In 2021 Ernst & Young surveyed more than 1,000 workers who had left their jobs during the Great Resignation and found that 58% cited a lack of empathy from their managers as a central cause of their departure. Increasingly employees, especially Millennials and Gen Zers, don't merely hope for empathy from their leaders—they demand it.

But for all its virtues, empathic leadership can be emotionally exhausting. Imagine wearing an empathy helmet that transmits the feelings of the people you work with into your head and heart. When you adopt empathy in the workplace, you expose yourself to the emotional ups and downs of everyone you manage—a welter of joy, anxiety, anger, self-doubt, fear, confusion, exuberance, jealousy, sadness, disappointment, and more. The 2020s, with all their challenges, have left employees stressed, exhausted, and pushed to the brink. When the people around us suffer, the empathy helmet becomes much heavier.

It's possible to absorb only so much. A 2022 survey from Future Forum found that middle managers report more burnout than do workers of any other type. Empathy can even take a physical toll: One academic study found that while teenagers of empathic parents report less depression than their peers do, those parents show more cellular signs of aging than other parents do. In being empathic, it seems, they help their kids but hurt themselves.

A need to practice empathy may also increase self-criticism. For leaders it can become another item on the to-do list to be fretted over. Recently a friend of mine, who works as an executive at a *Fortune* 100 technology firm and is brimming with empathy, confessed that he constantly second-guesses his caring. "I feel like I'm never enough," he said, "even in my empathy for my people. Anything going wrong with them means I've failed."

Not surprisingly, given the costs, some managers believe they must make a choice: be empathic and sacrifice their own well-being for the good of others, or back away emotionally and leave their people high and dry. Fortunately, this dilemma is more imagined than real. You can employ three strategies to manage your caring as a leader, which together form a practice I call *sustainable empathy*. In this article, drawing on my experience as a psychologist and a neuroscientist, I'll describe those strategies.

Compassion Fatigue

Much of what I've learned about sustainable empathy comes from spending time with health care professionals. Especially in emergency and critical-care settings, physicians, nurses, and social

HOW TO SUSTAIN YOUR EMPATHY IN DIFFICULT TIMES

Idea in Brief

The Challenge

Employees of all types are burned-out and desperately need empathy from their managers. But empathic leadership can be so emotionally and physically draining that it feels unsustainable.

The Dilemma

Many managers believe they have to make a choice: be empathic

and sacrifice their well-being for the good of others, or back away to preserve their own emotional health.

The Solution

This dilemma is less real than it seems. Three strategies—discussed in detail in this article—can help managers lead empathically over the long term without burning out.

workers encounter a stream of people who are having the worst days of their lives. These workers drink from a fire hose of human misery, go home to care for their own families, and then return to do it all over again.

That takes a toll. Three decades ago the nurse Carla Joinson first described "compassion fatigue," an affliction common among those in her profession who cared so much for patients that their emotions ran dry. When we're chronically exposed to the suffering of others, we experience fatigue, which in turn leads to burnout, defined as a general loss of meaning and connection. Both fatigue and burnout skyrocketed among caregivers during the Covid-19 pandemic. Today more than half of all nurses report severe burnout—an epidemic on its own.

In the so-called caring professions, such as medicine and teaching, empathy has long been at the heart of people's work—and has often become an occupational hazard. Nurses and doctors experience an intense form of this problem, but many workplace managers experience something similar. The need to empathize with struggling employees can leave them emotionally ragged, making it harder for them to do their jobs well. Nevertheless, over the years I've met nurses and physicians who manage to be both stalwart in their connection to patients and hardy and healthy themselves. Here are the three strategies I've discerned.

1. Physician, Heal Thyself

You doubtless wouldn't look to a regular smoker for advice about how to quit, or to someone with a messy home for tips on tidying up. The ancient proverb "Physician, heal thyself" signals that we shouldn't trust people to help us who can't help themselves. Some health care workers I've observed are laser-focused on doing everything they can for patients and families but rarely think about or take care of themselves. I once shadowed a doctor for six hours and only later realized that she hadn't eaten, drunk water, sat down, or used the bathroom all day. Other health care workers *do* think about self-care—but only as a sign of weakness. "If I have any little piece of energy left at the end of the day," one told me, "then I didn't do all I could."

This way of thinking, which we might call a "martyr mentality," is common among empathic managers. To avoid feeling selfish, many of them absorb the stress others are suffering. And some wear the martyr mentality like a badge of honor. But if they fail to care for themselves, can they be relied on to support the well-being of their reports?

Experiencing extreme stress isn't just painful; it also harms your ability to truly be there for your people. Stress numbs you to others' concerns, makes it harder to see the world through their eyes, and may even make you more aggressive. In one recent study in *Personnel Psychology* 112 managers were surveyed over 10 consecutive workdays. The more that people vented to their managers, the researchers found, the more negative emotion the managers felt the following day—which predicted that they were likely to mistreat others on their teams. When you let yourself burn out, you deny everyone else the best version of yourself.

The good news is that caring for yourself is the opposite of selfish: It's a vital path to sustainable empathy. Research on college students, workers, and long-term mediators has shown that people who care for themselves tend to be deliberate in their connections to others. And recent studies of social-service providers and business students have shown that practicing "self-compassion," in particular, protects people from exhaustion.

Self-compassion, which draws on Buddhist techniques for coping with suffering, was brought to modern behavioral science by the psychologist Kristen Neff. It involves three steps: cultivating awareness of what you're going through; focusing on "common humanity," which involves recognizing that suffering is universal; and establishing goodwill by extending kindness and grace to yourself.

These practices are powerful. Research finds that people high in self-compassion tend to be mentally healthier than others, more able to control their emotions, and quicker to recover from setbacks. But few people appreciate its benefits. In a survey of about 400 college students, Neff found that the majority reported being kinder to others than they are to themselves. And in new research from my own lab, about half the people we surveyed believed that self-compassion makes one complacent and irresponsible. Those who held these negative beliefs were less likely to be kind to themselves after failures and to bounce back from them.

No matter what industry you're in, managing others well begins with managing yourself. You can do that in a few ways.

Acknowledge the distress that comes from caring about the pain of others

After talking with a struggling colleague, take stock of your own emotions. If the conversation left you drained or upset, give yourself some time to process it.

Treat yourself with the same grace you offer others

Like my friend the tech executive, you may feel that anything going wrong with your team is your fault. But if a friend came to you with the same problem, you probably wouldn't judge that person as harshly.

Don't be afraid to ask for help

Leaders often feel they have to project confidence and serenity no matter what. But as a leader you're a model for your team, and if you're willing to be vulnerable, others are likely to follow your example. That is good for everyone. Most workers are eager to help their colleagues, and teams with a culture of helping tend to be efficient, creative, and tight-knit. I've seen this in my lab, where we begin some meetings with attendees sharing something they could use help with—a practice that produces an avalanche of goodwill and openness. I know firsthand that leaders often have trouble admitting they could use support, but amazing things can happen when people in power overcome that reluctance and allow themselves to reveal how they feel.

2. Learn to Tune Your Caring

Over the course of my career, hundreds of people have confidently told me what empathy is—but their definitions of it have often differed. Does empathy mean walking a mile in someone else's shoes? Feeling what others feel? Being kind to them?

Some of this confusion arises because empathy isn't one thing at all. It encompasses multiple ways in which we connect with others. Two in particular matter for understanding burnout: *Emotional empathy* involves taking on someone else's feelings. *Empathic concern* involves wanting to improve someone else's well-being.

These forms of empathy are connected in some ways but diverge in others. For example, a person who tends to take on other people's feelings won't necessarily score high on empathic concern. Newborn babies and many animals show signs of emotional empathy; empathic concern is rarer in the animal kingdom and takes time to develop in children. There's a reason for this divergence: Research has shown that different forms of empathy are supported by different systems in the brain.

Crucially, when it comes to burnout, these two types of empathy are not created equal. For instance, doctors who are emotionally empathic (they tend to take on others' distress) are likelier to burn out than those high in empathic concern (they have an urge to help). We seem to understand this intuitively. People high in emotional empathy tend to avoid volunteering if it means encountering suffering people, while people high in empathic concern dive right in.

Often emotional empathy is simply not what others need from us: A manager who cries uncontrollably while you share your problems is unlikely to be very comforting or helpful. As one scholar of medical empathy writes, "Caring binds, but sharing blinds."

The lesson here is that you can tune in to different frequencies of empathy. Resilient health-care workers do that in two ways: In difficult moments they calibrate their emotions, keeping their empathic concern high and their emotional empathy relatively low; and they create space for patients' emotions, pay close attention, and offer comfort while also maintaining some boundaries. This is often what patients want. In *The Empathy Exams,* the writer Leslie Jamison describes her time as a medical actor who would pantomime symptoms for doctors in training and rate their responses to her. Jamison imagined that emotional connection would matter—and it did. But the *kind* of connection mattered as well. She most appreciated students who were present but didn't take on her (pretend) distress. Describing one student who did this well, she writes, "His calmness didn't make me feel abandoned: it made me feel secure," adding, "I needed to look at him and see the opposite of my fear, not its echo."

You can help yourself and the people you work with by tuning yourself toward concern and away from distress. In a recent study psychologists surveyed more than 2,000 *Harvard Business Review* readers in leadership positions, along with more than 1,000 of the people they manage. The leaders were given hypothetical scenarios in which people on their teams were struggling and were asked the extent to which they would respond by trying to take on the feelings of an individual (emotional empathy) or to express caring for that person (empathic concern). Leaders who focused on concern were less burned-out, more effective in their work, and less likely to want to leave their jobs. Furthermore, the positive effects of concern reverberated: Employees who worked with those leaders rated them as particularly caring and competent.

In other words, empathy doesn't just connect people; it helps us lead more effectively. This advantage is driven by empathic concern and is especially strong during difficult moments. In one study researchers examined 360-degree reviews conducted at a large Canadian company, focusing on negative feedback from managers. Such performance conversations are never fun—and they can be exhausting for managers who take on others' distress. But when managers high in empathic concern provided feedback, the people who reported to them were more likely than their colleagues to appreciate it. And those managers were more likely to be viewed as promotable by their bosses. Empathic concern can convert challenging moments into opportunities to connect.

That doesn't mean emotional empathy has no place. Years ago my colleague Sylvia Morelli and I asked people to complete this sentence: "I feel empathy when someone else feels _____." Respondents named negative emotions 40 times as often as positive ones. That's common: Most people think of empathy as a portal into others' pain. But it can—and should—also be a portal into their joy. I've seen firsthand that wise health-care workers remember to ride emotional highs with patients and families, replenishing their own reserves for the inevitable lows. When you can share the joy people are feeling, your empathy helmet doesn't exhaust you; it energizes you.

We can all benefit from tuning our caring more intentionally. Begin by asking yourself, "What kind of empathy do I want to bring to this situation?" Consider what your colleagues need from you and what you need to keep going without burning out. Probably you'll realize that empathic concern, rather than emotional empathy, aligns with the needs of everyone involved and with your values as a leader. In those moments try to manage your own emotional landscape. Acknowledge your colleagues' suffering but don't get stuck in it. A minute of deep breathing can help. At the same time, lean into empathic concern and goodwill. Think about—maybe even write down—how you'd like your colleagues' well-being to improve and what you can do to help.

In other cases you may realize that emotional empathy is appropriate. When wins occur, no matter how small or rare, savor them with your employees and create ways for them to celebrate one another, using shared feeling to bring your team closer.

3. Remember That Empathy Is a Skill

Take a moment to think of the most and the least empathic people you've ever known. Then ask yourself how they got to be the way they are. You might find that question nonsensical if you believe that empathy—or a lack of it—is hardwired into us at birth. Many people seem to hold that belief: About a decade ago Carol Dweck, Karina Schumann, and I put the question to study participants and discovered that about half of them thought that people cannot change the degree of empathy they feel. If you share that view, you probably believe that sustainable empathy is out of reach.

Fortunately, decades' worth of evidence demonstrates that empathy is more like a skill than a trait. Yes, some people are born more empathic than others, but sustainable empathy is within your grasp. Furthermore, Carol, Karina, and I have found that when people understand empathy as a skill, they work harder at practicing it. Much of my work over the past five years has focused on empowering people and organizations with this knowledge, showing them practical tools for building empathy and helping them understand that difficult times in an organization are not challenges you have to avoid; they are opportunities for growth.

When you understand that empathy can be developed, you also understand that caring *well* doesn't always mean caring *more*. With that in mind, Eve Ekman, a social worker and a behavioral scientist who studies contemplative practices such as meditation, has developed trainings in which "emotional balance" is the goal: People learn not how to become more or less empathic but, rather, how to adjust their empathy to account for self-compassion as well as concern for others. The biologist and Buddhist monk Matthieu Ricard describes meditating himself into a state of pure emotional empathy—and nearly collapsing in anguish. For relief he brought himself into a state of empathic concern.

Few of us are monks, but early research suggests that tactics similar to Ricard's can make empathy sustainable—especially "metta," or "compassion meditation." This practice involves focusing your attention first on yourself and then on other people and repeating expressions of goodwill toward them, such as "May you be peaceful" and "May you be safe from harm." That may sound wacky, but compassion meditation can enhance your ability to connect with others and even change your brain in the process. It can be a powerful tool for people whose jobs require caring. In one study medical students who practiced compassion meditation reported stronger connections with their patients but fewer symptoms of depression than other med students did.

Strive to become more aware of how you empathize. The next time a colleague is upset, run an internal audit: To what degree did you take on the other person's feelings rather than demonstrate goodwill or attempt to take your colleague's perspective? It's also important to practice tuning your caring, whether in the moment or, better yet, beforehand. If you know a tough conversation is coming up, try to "preregulate" yourself with a few minutes of mindfulness. Instead of getting sucked in by another's feelings, focus on what you want for your colleague in the long term and how you can help achieve that.

Our tumultuous times have saturated organizations with anxiety and exhaustion. Employees of all types are burned out and desperately need empathy from their leaders. But leaders are burned out too, and may feel as if they're pouring from an empty cup. Fortunately, through the right practices—self-compassion, empathic tuning, and building healthy habits of mind—managers and employees alike can make their empathy sustainable. These practices are key to becoming the leaders most of us aspire to be. So when in doubt, find new ways to be there for yourself. In the long run, it's the best way to be there for everyone else.

Originally published in January–February 2024. Reprint R2401C

The New-Collar Workforce

by Colleen Ammerman, Boris Groysberg,
and Ginni Rometty

EARNING A BACHELOR'S DEGREE can expand one's mind, widen horizons, and provide a pathway to a well-paying, satisfying career. Yet for those who don't complete four years of college, the lack of a BA or BS looms as a barrier. Millions of people are locked out of promising job opportunities because too many companies default to hiring workers with four-year degrees, even for positions that don't require that level of education. The trend began decades ago but spiked during the Great Recession: Research by Alicia Sasser Modestino, Daniel Shoag, and Joshua Ballance shows that from 2007 to 2010, job postings requiring at least a bachelor's degree increased by 10%. That number dropped somewhat as the economy recovered, but scores of jobs remain inaccessible to people who have the skills and aptitude to succeed at them—but not a college diploma.

Unnecessary degree requirements don't just hurt workers. They also deprive companies of talent while yielding little to no benefit. Hiring managers may think that a bachelor's degree serves as a good proxy for things like collaboration skills, a sense of initiative, and the ability to think critically, but there's virtually no evidence to support that notion. In fact, when a team from Harvard Business School and Accenture recently analyzed "middle skill" jobs (which require some education or training beyond high school but not a four-year degree), they found no boosts in productivity when those jobs were done by college graduates.

Companies that use the bachelor's degree as a filter when filling positions that don't require it are hiring inefficiently. They're also overlooking workers they desperately need, particularly in growing fields such as tech, where the demand for people with specialized skills far outstrips the supply. At a time when many employers are struggling to fill vacancies and retain their current workforce, a gate-keeping mechanism with no proven benefit creates a competitive disadvantage.

Moreover, degree requirements undermine organizational commitments to improving racial diversity. Although U.S. Census data from 2021 shows that a majority (about 65%) of Americans who are 25 or older do not have a bachelor's, the proportions are highest among Black Americans (72%), indigenous populations (80%), and those who identify as Hispanic or Latinx (79%). An unnecessary insistence on credentials is, in short, blocking employers' access to a diverse, capable pool of talent, and the workers who are taking the biggest hit are those who are already marginalized.

It's no secret that we're living in a time of profound economic inequality. Workers and occupations are increasingly concentrated at the low and high ends of the economic ladder. The middle class in the United States is hollowing out, and a raft of research across multiple disciplines has found that this is perpetuating racial disparities, tearing the social fabric, and undermining democracy. It's time to fix our broken approach to talent management, for the good of not just workers and companies but also society as a whole.

We three have long been deeply compelled by questions about how companies find, treat, and support the employees who are at the core of any business. Colleen directs Harvard Business School's Race, Gender & Equity (RGE) Initiative, which aims to eradicate racial and gender-based disparities and other forms of inequality in organizations and society at large. Boris has been researching and teaching about effective hiring and retention, and about managing for diversity, equity, and inclusion, for more than 20 years, and he is a faculty affiliate at the RGE Initiative. And Ginni is a former CEO of

Idea in Brief

The Problem

Many jobs are inaccessible to workers who have the skills and aptitude to succeed at them—but not the four-year degree that employers often require. This situation is hurting workers, companies, and society as a whole.

The Faulty Mindset

Some hiring managers think that a bachelor's degree serves as a good proxy for capabilities such as collaborating well, taking initiative, and thinking critically. There's virtually no evidence to support that notion.

The Solution

A skills-based (rather than a degree-based) approach to hiring, promotion, and development offers companies a powerful means of meeting their staffing needs, advancing overlooked talent, and increasing racial and socioeconomic diversity.

IBM who expanded opportunities there for people of diverse backgrounds and who now serves as a cochair of OneTen, a coalition of employers committed to hiring Black workers without four-year degrees into family-sustaining jobs.

Collectively we've written several books that address talent, diversity, and effective management, most recently Ginni's *Good Power: Leading Positive Change in Our Lives, Work, and World* (Harvard Business Review Press, 2023). Together, we recently interviewed leaders in various industries about their companies' talent management practices. What they told us confirms our own prior research and real-world experience: There's a straightforward, practical way that firms can foster prosperity and diversity while also unlocking a huge and capable talent pool. The secret is focusing on skills.

Skills-First Hiring

Ten years ago IBM, like many other organizations, was struggling to fill some key jobs. At the same time, it was increasingly clear that the benefits of the burgeoning tech industry were not accruing equally across society. Indeed, many people were more likely to see technology as a threat to their livelihood than as a field where they could climb the economic ladder. And no wonder: Well-paying tech jobs were largely out of reach for those without a bachelor's degree. At IBM in 2012, less than 10% of U.S.-based roles were open to such applicants, regardless of their other qualifications. Ginni, who was then the CEO, knew that a different approach was needed.

To widen its excessively narrow talent funnel, the company launched what Ginni referred to as the SkillsFirst initiative: IBM overhauled its hiring practices to create on-ramps for people who were previously overlooked and to build a pipeline of capable non-degreed workers. For any organization with the same goals, the process involves action on multiple fronts.

Building a new taxonomy of skills

At IBM, HR teams reevaluated job descriptions and worked with business units throughout the company to find out what knowledge and expertise was needed for specific roles. Rather than assume that applicants with college degrees possessed relevant capabilities—and that those without college degrees did not—the teams studied all open positions, identified the genuinely requisite skills, and then rewrote job descriptions accordingly, emphasizing specific abilities over general credentials. For example, a cybersecurity job posting once would have listed the experience and degrees required. Now it lists desired skills and attributes and focuses on the core capabilities needed to do the job, such as being able to develop hypotheses and apply programming languages.

As companies revise job postings, they have to be careful to avoid language that might suggest a bias against applicants who don't come from privileged backgrounds. "You can remove the degree requirement," says Obed Louissaint, who led talent at IBM until recently, "but if you include 'experience traveling,' that may turn off a candidate."

Crafting job descriptions is also best done as a joint effort, with input from HR, hiring managers, and experienced supervisors. Mindful of that, IBM created an "enterprise skills team" consisting of a dozen senior and emerging leaders who together identified the most important qualifications for a range of entry-level roles. They included hard skills that were specific to particular jobs and soft skills important in all of them. Developing and maintaining a database of this kind is vital for skills-first hiring, but according to a 2022 report by LinkedIn Learning, only 10% of organizations actually do it. External experts can help. Cleveland Clinic, for example, worked with the diversity-strategy firm Grads of Life to analyze more than 400 roles, representing 20,000 total jobs, and then revised degree and credential requirements to remove unnecessary qualifications. The effort was so successful that the clinic expanded its skills analysis to thousands of additional roles.

Broadening the talent pool

To develop a successful skills-first hiring practice, companies should provide on-ramps—such as apprenticeships, internships, and training programs—for people who have aptitude but are untraditional candidates. It can be tempting to frame these mechanisms as altruistic efforts or to consider them the domain of corporate social-responsibility units. But such a view is backward, according to Greg Case, the CEO of Aon, a risk management firm. He says that if business leaders are "asking how we give people access to our companies, that is the wrong question. The real question is, How can we equip *ourselves* to access this talent?"

Aon offered its first apprenticeship opportunities in finance, IT, and human resources—all departments that were experiencing high attrition. It partnered with City Colleges of Chicago to establish a program in which apprentices combine relevant courses with part-time work at the company, with the goal of earning associate's degrees and ultimately transitioning into full-time employment. Aon has benefited in multiple ways: It has filled vacancies, brought more people of color into the company, and seen higher retention rates for employees hired through the apprentice program than for those hired directly from college.

One way that IBM grew its tech talent pool was by creating internships for students and graduates of a program known as P-TECH (Pathways in Technology Early College High School). The program enables students to take classes in STEM fields and earn credits toward an associate's degree in applied science while completing high school. It started as a partnership among IBM, the City University of New York, and the New York City Department of Education and was launched in a single Brooklyn high school in 2011. Since then it has expanded rapidly: In 2022 more than 300 P-TECH schools in 27 countries provided interns, apprentices, and employees to businesses worldwide. Employing students and graduates of P-TECH has been a key element of IBM's talent strategy.

Reimagining existing relationships

Assessing how well an organization is leveraging existing educational institutions and talent developers can be just as transformative as starting up a new program. When Cleveland Clinic, the largest employer in its region, embarked on its skills-first journey, it shifted the way it engaged with local training providers to build new pathways into its workforce. Historically, for example, it had hired graduates of health care training programs if they had prior hospital experience. That meant that people might complete such training programs but still face limited job prospects. Today Cleveland Clinic hires graduates with and without prior hospital experience and invests in upskilling the latter.

Retraining managers

Hiring managers are a critical part of the skills-first equation. It's crucial to stop them from using traditional degrees or prior work experience as proxies for a candidate's capability. To help managers effectively assess applicants for jobs that don't require degrees, companies need to give them appropriate tools—including standardized, job-relevant evaluation rubrics—and train them to recognize interviewer biases.

Companies can also redesign hiring processes to more accurately size up people's skills. In many situations it's already common to test for technical knowledge, but softer skills can be evaluated too—with problem-solving exercises, "job auditions" (wherein candidates undertake a task or project), and other innovative methods that help hiring managers focus on someone's mindset and abilities.

Managers may be more motivated to hire nondegreed workers—and feel that it's less risky—if they have direct incentives to do so. For instance, companies can provide extra funding or budget lines for such hires. Peer modeling, too, can encourage managers to embrace skills-first approaches. Seeing is believing, after all. After working with the U.S. Department of Labor to design an apprenticeship program suitable for modern information-technology jobs, IBM brought in a cohort of seven apprentices in 2017. A software team leader volunteered to host the apprentices, who quickly became known as strong performers and eager learners. Within months, other teams and business units were requesting apprentices, and demand grew. By 2020 the program had expanded to more than 20 IT roles.

Managers who see the value of tapping into an overlooked talent pool, and who hence demand access to it, are the key to truly embedding skills-first hiring in an organization. As Aon's Case explains, "Frontline leaders who recognize that there is a source of talent they have not had access to are the engine. The CEO push and the HR push are important, but it's the managers who are going to create sustainability when they see that they can bring this talent in and do great work."

Scaling appropriately

It may be tempting to start small and hire a few people one by one as a kind of viability test. However, the company leaders we have spoken to about their skills-first hiring efforts were unanimous and definitive: A tentative approach is counterproductive.

The cohort experience is critical for both nontraditional hires and the colleagues they join. New employees without four-year degrees need to see that the organization is investing in workers like them, not timidly experimenting around the edges. And in an environment where they may fear being viewed as unqualified or feel out of place, having a community of similar peers can bolster confidence and connection. Hiring a sizable cohort also reinforces to the company at large that skills-first approaches are integral, not superfluous. One or two people are likely to languish if they don't seamlessly fit into an organizational culture where their value is underrecognized, but a robust cohort can precipitate changes to the culture itself.

Companies shouldn't expect workers hired through a skills-first approach to assimilate to their new environment without appropriate support. Leaders should therefore update their corporate norms and practices to embed skills-first thinking throughout talent management. That's how they'll get the most from both their new employees and their existing workforce.

A Skills-Based Culture

Fundamentally, a skills-first approach is about building rather than buying talent. Creating entry points and on-ramps for newcomers of varied backgrounds is an important first step. But by taking a skills-based approach to promotion and development for *all* employees, companies can advance overlooked talent and increase racial and socioeconomic diversity in the entire workforce and the leadership pipeline.

Internal pathways to jobs with higher pay and more responsibility are critical. At Delta Air Lines, frontline employees can train for jobs in the company's analytics group through a program that sponsors their enrollment in relevant coursework at Georgia State University, or they can opt to pursue pilot training through a program known as Propel. Similarly, Bank of America runs what it calls the Academy, which provides education and skill-building opportunities for all employees so that they can pursue new jobs within and across functions. In 2021 more than 65,000 people took advantage of the Academy's training and development programs. Career mobility is core to the company's talent strategy: Whereas about 30% of vacant jobs at the bank were formerly filled by internal hires, in 2021 more than 50% were.

Harnessing the power of a skills-centric approach requires a paradigm shift in how firms think about talent. Maurice Jones, the CEO of OneTen (whose members include all the companies cited as examples in this article), argues that most organizations counterproductively cultivate a narrow and even exclusionary "image of excellence." Too often that prevents their managers from accurately appreciating the value that people without a four-year degree may bring to the table, especially if they're Black or from another marginalized and underestimated group. To thwart that tendency, IBM began using the term "new-collar workers" to signal respect for workers who do not have a college diploma but are just as talented and capable as their degreed counterparts.

Skills-first talent management will be successful only if it is undertaken as a companywide initiative. Individual managers can't be expected to make it happen on their own. They need backing from top leaders who are ready for skeptics and willing to meet them with full-throated support for a skills focus. The OneTen member companies making the most progress toward their shared goal, Jones says, are those "where the CEO is visibly committed and treating it like any other business priority."

When we've talked to chief executives at companies leaning in to skills-first talent management, all have echoed the need to elevate and legitimize what is essentially a cultural transformation. Tomislav Mihaljevic, the CEO of Cleveland Clinic, told us that he's tried to make sure that everybody in his organization understands the "why." A skills-first approach, he says, "cannot be 'mandated' in the classical sense of the word. It has to be explained. Ultimately the only way for culture to stick and for these changes to become permanent is if they get embraced by the entire organization, not just a chosen few." Brian Moynihan, the CEO of Bank of America, makes a slightly different point, noting that leaders must ensure that managers have the latitude and support to make the necessary changes to their processes, even if that takes time and involves inefficiencies at first. "I have to drive a culture that embraces this as a way of doing business," he says.

Investing in the careers of employees is a surefire way to increase engagement and retention, and a culture of such investment positively impacts all workers, regardless of their degree status. At the height of the Covid-19 pandemic, Delta found that Black employees, including those in mid- and senior-level jobs, were leaving at higher rates than others. According to Ed Bastian, the CEO, the company had tried to diversify its pipeline prior to the pandemic by bringing in experienced Black talent, but those workers were less invested than longer-tenured employees. When the pandemic threw the industry into turmoil, they felt little motivation to stick with the company. Today Delta focuses not just on diversifying its overall workforce but also on cultivating internal talent, paying particular attention to members of groups that historically had limited advancement opportunities. In addition to its analytics and Propel offerings, the company maintains an apprenticeship program to offer existing employees on-the-job training in 74 different roles. The program has seen enormous demand from workers eager to expand their skills and advance.

Bank of America also offers internal training opportunities to help employees move up. To track the outcomes of its learning and development programs, the company is assembling a dashboard of turnover and promotion rates by cohort that allows leaders to see race and gender patterns as well as overall trends. "Measuring how many people go through a development program is one thing," Moynihan says, "but what you really should be measuring is how many people who went through that program are being promoted to the next level."

Not all upskilling needs to be done in-house. Through robust relationships with community colleges and other talent-development institutions, companies can help ensure that people who pursue such training and education are learning the right skills. Aon's partnership with City Colleges of Chicago includes updating and adapting curricula so that apprentices' coursework is job-relevant. Bank of America provides a career-development curriculum to community colleges, workforce development organizations, and other nonprofits, enabling students to be hired more quickly into professional jobs.

A skills-first culture is also about understanding what workers need to be successful and achieve their full potential. That might include easy access to their workplaces and flexible scheduling. Individual companies may not be able to remedy societal problems like deficiencies in transportation infrastructure and shortages of childcare facilities—which are especially likely to be barriers to employment for nondegreed workers—but they can look for creative solutions. For instance, Merck realized that for the primarily Black Philadelphia residents whom it wanted to hire, commuting via public transportation to its manufacturing facility in suburban West Point was challenging and probably unsustainable. To improve access to the city's talent pool, as well as meet other business needs, the company opened a new facility in Philadelphia.

Ultimately, a skills-first approach will yield the greatest benefit if organizations extend it beyond hiring and make it core to how they think about cultivating and retaining talent. At Aon the success of apprenticeships for back-office roles spurred the addition of apprenticeships in risk management, actuarial science, and investment consulting—jobs at the center of the firm's mission. The Chicago Apprentice Network, which Aon formed in 2017 with Accenture and the insurance company Zurich North America, has grown to include more than 90 companies that understand the merits of an apprenticeship approach.

A Skills-First Future

The need for skills-first talent management is clear. Capable employees are out there, sometimes with a sight line to a satisfying, well-paid job but often with no realistic way to get there.

Consider Tony, who in 2018 was working at a coffee shop at IBM's Durham, North Carolina, location. Every day he served the office employees who streamed onto and off the campus. It was dispiriting but also inspiring. "Coming to IBM every single day," he said, "I'm thinking, *Man, it would be nice to actually work for IBM. Instead, I have to work in this coffee shop. But there's probably no way unless I go to school for four years.*"

A high school graduate and the father of young children, Tony simply didn't have time for that. Then he learned about IBM's apprenticeship opportunities from a customer. He applied, did a yearlong apprenticeship, and ultimately landed a full-time technical position in customer support.

He now has a sense of future possibilities at IBM. "My manager started out as an L2 engineer," he told us, "where I'm at now. Maybe one day I can climb my way up and become a manager—someone that's able to lead the team or lead a few different teams. Building up as high as I can go."

For too long, four-year-degree requirements have been easy, if ineffective, shortcuts that made managers feel they were weeding out less qualified talent. Data and time have proven this assumption false. What's more, it artificially constrains companies' efforts to advance racial diversity, cultivate employee engagement, and generate strong performance.

Companies can do better—for workers and themselves—by embracing skills-based talent management. Making the switch takes time and investment, but the costs are worth it. A skills-based approach promises better matching between job candidates and jobs, dramatically expands talent pools, improves internal mobility and employee commitment, and incentivizes HR departments and business units to stay aware of what each job actually entails. This approach also holds the potential to mitigate the economic and racial inequalities that are fracturing U.S. society and compromising the health of its institutions and economy.

Organizations do not exist apart from the communities and regions in which they are situated. Mihaljevic highlighted that idea when describing why he and his team have adopted a skills-first approach: "Unless the community around us thrives, Cleveland Clinic cannot thrive. It is essential for Cleveland Clinic's success and sustainability in the future that we create opportunities for the people who live here."

Originally published in March–April 2023. Reprint R2302G

Rid Your Organization of Obstacles That Infuriate Everyone

by Robert I. Sutton and Huggy Rao

IN AUGUST 1940, AS HIS COUNTRY prepared for waves of attacks by German planes, Britain's prime minister, Winston Churchill, set out to address a different enemy: lengthy reports. In his 234-word "Brevity" memo, he implored the members of his war cabinet and their staffs to "see to it that their reports are shorter." Churchill urged them to write "short, crisp paragraphs," to move complex arguments or statistics to appendices, and to stop using "officialese jargon."

We devoted eight years to learning about how leaders like Churchill serve as trustees of others' time—how they prevent or remove organizational obstacles that undermine the zeal, damage the health, and throttle the creativity and productivity of good people. We call our work "the Friction Project." It consists of our own research, case studies, workshops, and classes; interviews with 22 guests on our *Friction* podcast; hundreds of interactions with our sprawling network of leaders, researchers, and other savvy people; and an analysis of the academic and practical work of others.

Along the way, we learned that friction can be both bad and good: Not everything ought to be quick, easy, and frictionless. Activities that involve good friction include developing deep and trusting relationships, making complex and irreversible decisions under uncertainty, and doing creative work that's messy, inefficient, and failure-ridden (if you're doing it right!). Skilled leaders are bent on eliminating unnecessary obstacles, in large part because doing so gives them more time to focus on those many things in organizational life that should be slow, hard, and complicated. (See the sidebar "What Ought to Be Easy or Hard in Your Company?")

In this article we focus on *addition sickness*: the unnecessary rules, procedures, communications, tools, and roles that seem to inexorably grow, stifling productivity and creativity. We show why companies are prone to this affliction and how leaders can treat it. The first step is to do a *good-riddance review* to identify obstacles that can and should be removed. The next step is to employ *subtraction tools* to eliminate those obstacles or make it difficult for people to add them in the first place. This article unpacks both steps.

Why Companies Are Plagued by Addition Sickness

Our project uncovered three forces that fuel these behaviors. First, we humans default to asking, "What can I add here?" and not "What can I get rid of?" Studies by Gabrielle Adams and her colleagues discussed in a 2021 *Nature* article found that this "addition bias" shapes the solutions that people generate to improve universities, edit their own and others' writing, modify soup recipes, plan trips, and build Lego creations. When one university president asked students, faculty, and staff members for suggestions to improve the place, only 11% of the responses entailed subtraction.

Second, organizations often reward leaders for additions: Kudos, cash, perks, and titles are heaped on those who implement new technologies, launch initiatives, or build bigger fiefdoms. In contrast, people with the wisdom and discipline to avoid adding unnecessary stuff are rarely noticed or rewarded. These incentives help explain why, although many of us believe that other people need to engage in subtraction, we object to eliminating our own pet projects or reducing our own budgets. As the late, great comedian George Carlin put it, "Have you noticed that their stuff is shit and your shit is stuff?"

Idea in Brief

The Problem

Virtually all organizations are plagued by addition sickness: the unnecessary rules, procedures, communications, tools, and roles that seem to inexorably grow, stifling productivity and creativity.

The Root Cause

People default to asking, "What can I add here?", not "What can I get rid of?" Organizations reward leaders for additions—implementing new technologies,

launching initiatives, building bigger fiefdoms. And leaders often have a limited grasp of their "cone of friction"—how their actions and decisions burden others.

The Remedy

Conduct a good-riddance review to identify obstacles that can and should be removed. And employ subtraction tools to eliminate those obstacles or make it difficult for people to erect them in the first place.

Third, leaders often have a limited grasp of their "cone of friction"—how their actions and decisions burden others. Part of the reason for such friction blindness, as Dacher Keltner's book *The Power Paradox* documents, is that when people feel powerful, they tend to focus more on what they need and want and less on the challenges and inconveniences faced by others (especially people who are less powerful than they are).

So leaders may not realize how their failure to remove, or to avoid adding, unnecessary impediments makes life harder for "the little people." At Stanford University, for example, a senior administrator sent a 1,266-word email with a 7,266-word attachment to more than 2,000 faculty members, inviting all of us to devote a Saturday to brainstorming about a new sustainability school. Apparently it never occurred to her that the email could have been trimmed by at least 500 words and the attachment by thousands of words. Such edits would have saved time for thousands of people in her cone of friction.

The good news is that leaders can do much to reverse addition sickness. They can begin by turning attention to identifying what can be removed (or not added). Gabrielle Adams's team found that when people paused to consider solutions or were reminded to

What Ought to Be Easy or Hard in Your Company?

NOT ALL INEFFICIENCIES ARE BAD. Many challenges in organizational life—making tough trade-offs, building deep and enduring relationships, accomplishing creative work, deciding to adopt measures that would heap yet more burdens on employees and customers—often are best dealt with slowly and by difficult and sometimes complicated methods. Eliminating friction in those situations can be soul-crushing for the people who do the work and can undermine productivity, safety, innovation, and commitment. Answering the following five questions can help you decide where to remove versus inject organizational friction.

1. Are you certain or uncertain about the right things to do?

In his book *Thinking, Fast and Slow,* Nobel Prize winner Daniel Kahneman argues that when people are in a "cognitive minefield"—when they are confused or overwhelmed, or when things are falling apart—it's wisest to pause and assess the situation rather than do something rash. When you find yourself in such circumstances, implore your people to slow down and think about the right thing to do. A CEO who led an impressive turnaround at a multinational explained to us that when a leader takes charge of a troubled company, "you have to assess the situation rather than act quickly." The CEO continued, "Everyone wants you to do something, so the first thing you say, very calmly, is, 'We're not going to do anything today.'"

2. Are you doing routine or creative work?

The best routine processes, such as getting an expense request approved or canceling a magazine subscription, are so frictionless that, to paraphrase the IDEO cofounder Bill Moggridge, you notice that you don't notice using them. In contrast, creative work requires constant struggle, frustration, confusion, and failure. There are ways to make creativity less inefficient—such as pulling the plug on bad ideas faster. But piles of studies show that streamlining creativity too much will kill it. As the psychologist Dean Keith Simonton has noted, geniuses such as Picasso, da Vinci, and Richard Feynman had far more successes *and failures* than their unheralded colleagues. In every occupation Simonton studied, including composer, artist, and inventor, "the most successful creators tend to be those with the most failures!"

3. Will the fast eat the slow, or is it better to pause and learn from others' mistakes?

Sometimes life is like a mousetrap: The first mouse gets crushed and the second (or third or fourth) mouse gets the cheese. Research on launching new businesses and products, for example, shows that the so-called first-mover advantage is sometimes a myth. When markets are treacherous and uncertainty is high, first movers often flounder because consumers aren't ready for their ideas yet or are put off by flawed early offerings. Companies that launch their products or services later win, in part, because they learn from the missteps of antsy early movers. Amazon, for example, wasn't the first online bookstore; the defunct Books.com and Interloc were earlier entrants.

4. Do people have the bandwidth to take on more work, or are they overextended or burned-out?

Too much of a good thing can be terrible. One exasperated service rep showed us that to serve just one customer, she had to switch among at least 15 applications and 20 windows on the 13-inch screen of her laptop. Her company had adopted so many efficiency tools to "help" its workers that it rendered them inefficient. Making it harder for that rep's IT team to add apps would have reduced her digital exhaustion.

5. Is your goal to develop quick but shallow or deep and enduring working relationships?

Teams of strangers with well-trained members who understand their roles can develop "cognitive trust" swiftly, which enables them to do good work—such as flight crews on commercial airlines and teams of doctors and nurses in emergency departments who have never met but perform complicated tasks together. Yet the best work happens after collaborators develop deep "emotional trust," which requires working, talking, and failing and succeeding together over long stretches of time. That's why teams and networks of people who start new companies, develop products, do surgery, and put on Broadway musicals perform better when they have worked together again and again. Sure, old teams can become stale and need injections of fresh blood. But it may take years before that becomes necessary. And some enduring relationships never lose their spark. Warren Buffett, the "oracle of Omaha," and Charlie Munger, his partner at Berkshire Hathaway, produced a remarkable record of financial performance for more than 50 years.

think about subtraction, they were less likely to default to addition. Venture capitalist Michael Dearing fires up this way of thinking by urging leaders to act as editors in chief of their organizations. He explains that, like skilled text and film editors, the best leaders relentlessly eliminate or repair things that distract, bore, bewilder, or exhaust people.

Good-Riddance Reviews

Savvy friction fixers assess what they should and can remove from their organizations and identify where and how to create mechanisms such as rules, review processes, and financial penalties that make it harder to add unnecessary stuff. Here are some methods they employ.

Ask colleagues and customers to identify unnecessary obstacles

When Melinda Ashton was the chief quality officer at Hawaii Pacific Health, the largest nonprofit health care system in the state, she was troubled because clinical staffers were devoting too much time to updating patients' electronic health records and too little time to examining, treating, and comforting patients.

To address the problem, Ashton and her team launched the Getting Rid of Stupid Stuff program in 2017 (yes, the acronym is GROSS). As Ashton reported in the *New England Journal of Medicine*, one of the first steps was to ask nurse assistants, nurses, and doctors to nominate anything in the system that "was poorly designed, unnecessary, or just plain stupid." Hawaii Pacific employees identified 188 subtraction targets, which sparked 87 improvements. Subtracting all that stupid stuff freed up a lot of time. In response to one nomination, Ashton's team eliminated a mouse click that every nurse and nurse assistant was required to make for every patient during hourly rounds. That saved 24 seconds per click—which, Ashton reports, "consumed approximately 1,700 nursing hours per month at our four hospitals."

You can also ask clients to identify subtraction targets. Our students Saul Gurdus and Elizabeth Woodson spent 10 weeks helping administrators at a California social services agency identify and remove pain points for clients—especially obstacles that caused unnecessary delay and despair among applicants. Gurdus and Woodson used client interviews to identify junctures in the application process—usually handoffs between silos—where clients reported "waiting" and "still waiting" and feeling "invisible" and "this is too hard." Then they worked with administrators to remove impediments to communication across silos, which, in turn, reduced waiting times and clients' frustration.

Calculate the burdens of performance measurement

Are you spending so much time evaluating one another that you don't have time to do your work? When Marcus Buckingham and Ashley Goodall crunched the numbers at the global services firm Deloitte, they discovered that the 65,000 employees were collectively spending nearly 2 million hours a year on performance management—completing the forms, attending meetings, and creating the ratings (see "Reinventing Performance Management," HBR, April 2015).

Assess the burden imposed by meetings

As part of the Friction Project, we worked with Rebecca Hinds, the head of Asana's Work Innovation Lab, on a "meeting reset" intervention with 60 Asana employees. We asked participants to rate the value and importance of each recurring meeting on their calendars. They assessed 1,160 standing meetings and identified more than 500 that were of low value. Hinds guided those colleagues to remove or revamp those meetings. As a result, on average, each employee saved more than four hours a month. Canceling meetings had the biggest impact (37% of total minutes saved). Making adjustments to format, such as scheduling meetings less often, shortening them, and relying more on written communication and less on presentations and conversations, accounted for the other 63%.

Catalog email overload

A 2019 Adobe survey of the email usage of 1,002 U.S. adults found that they spent, on average, more than five hours a day reading and responding to work email (three-plus hours) and personal email (two-plus hours). As John Lilly, the former CEO of Mozilla, put it to us, "After all these years, email is still the internet's killer app, and keeping up with it crushes productivity and creativity in every company I know." You can begin to fight back by reviewing the number, length, recipients, and timing of the emails that people send and receive and by developing solutions to lighten the load. A policy like the "zzzMail" rule instituted at the consulting firm Vynamic might help: Employees are asked not to send internal emails between 10 p.m. and 6 a.m. Monday through Friday, on weekends, and on all Vynamic holidays.

Count how many people report to each leader

An unfortunate side effect of flat structures is that executives sometimes have so many people reporting to them that their jobs become impossible. In *Beyond Collaboration Overload*, Rob Cross describes "Scott" as an executive who was "flying up the hierarchy" of a large company until he took charge of three big units—some 5,000 people. Scott had had just a few direct reports in past roles; he had 16 this time. He wanted to be "less hierarchical," so he urged people "to bring him problems and concerns or to include him in discussions."

By the time Cross was called in to help, Scott was working 16 hours a day, seven days a week, and still falling behind. When Cross examined the networks of the company's top 10,000 people, Scott "was the number 1 most overloaded person." Some 120 people came to him every day for information. Cross found that 78 of the 150 top managers in one unit Scott ran "felt they couldn't hit their business goals unless they got more of Scott's time."

Interview and observe users

Leaders at the nonprofit Civilla conducted more than 250 hours of interviews and observations with residents, civil servants, and leaders to identify needless and confusing questions on a benefits form. More than 2 million Michigan residents had to complete the convoluted document each year to apply for childcare, food, and health care support from the state. It contained 18,000 words and more than 1,000 questions—many of which were unnecessary and intrusive.

A turning point in Civilla's Project Re:form came when leaders met with executives from the Michigan Department of Health and Human Services (MDHHS), the organization responsible for the form, and asked them to fill it out. As a Civilla cofounder, Adam Selzer, told us, none of the executives had attempted to complete the 42-page form before. Terry Beurer, the department head at MDHHS, got no further than page eight before giving up. Beurer told Civilla's CEO, Michael Brennan, that it was among the most humbling experiences of his career. To Beurer's credit, rather than getting defensive and making excuses, he signed up for the project on the spot and provided his time and department resources throughout the challenging, but ultimately successful, four-year effort to drastically shrink the form.

Subtraction Tools

During our research for our book *The Friction Project,* we discovered an array of tools that help leaders rid their organizations of unnecessary burdens—and make it harder to add needless impediments in the first place. Savvy leaders experiment with different combinations of tools to develop the right portfolio for tackling their company's particular friction troubles.

Simple subtraction rules

Crisp constraints help people remove unnecessary impediments from organizations. One example is the rule implemented by Laszlo Bock when he led people operations at Google, which is "dedicated to staffing, development, and a distinct and inclusive culture." Bock told us that tremendous burdens had been heaped on employees and job candidates by the company's tradition of conducting eight to 12, and sometimes 25, rounds of interviews with a candidate before making an offer (or not). Bock responded with a simple rule: If more than four interviews were to be conducted with a candidate, the request for an exception had to be approved by him. It worked like a charm. The excessive rounds of interviews that exhausted employees and drove away good candidates disappeared instantly.

The "rule of halves" is another simple subtraction tool. We ask people to imagine how they could reduce each work burden by 50%—such as the number of standing meetings they attend, the length of the emails they send, the number of recommendations they require for new hires, and the number of digital collaboration tools they use. People rarely cut 50%, but they do reduce their workload.

That's what happened when Rob Cross coached Scott, that deeply overextended executive, and suggested that he cut back his direct reports, meetings, and emails by about 50%—targets that Scott actually hit. His direct reports felt more empowered (and less overloaded) because they made more decisions without checking and coordinating with him. And because Scott had fewer people to deal with—and resisted jumping into every decision—his unit operated more efficiently. He worked fewer hours, his health improved, and, Cross tells us, he saved his troubled marriage.

The subtraction game

We have played this game with more than 100 organizations. It starts with solo brainstorming. We ask people, "Think about how your organization operates. What adds needless frustration? What scatters your attention? What was once useful but is now in the way?" Next, people meet in small groups to discuss the impediments identified and name additional subtraction targets. Then they select two or three targets and outline rough implementation plans—who might lead the charge, whose support they would need, and which people or teams might quash the change. Some groups pick a practical idea (one CEO vowed to keep his emails under 500 words) and an impractical one (engineers proposed to disband HR). Others select something easy to subtract (one team reduced the number of communications apps it was using) and something tough (the members of a top team agreed that their company would run better and their mental health would improve if they removed two micromanagers from the board of directors).

Groups sometimes act on the spot. While playing the game with 25 colleagues at a software firm, one vice president disbanded a troubled project and shifted his weekly team meeting to every other week. The CEO of a financial services company jumped up and told his top 80 people that within a week he wanted an email from each of them with two subtraction targets. Within a month he wanted the changes implemented—and he offered each person a $5,000 bonus for making that happen. Nearly all 80 managers earned the bonus. Their changes included ending poorly performing product lines, eliminating meetings, and terminating contracts with unreliable vendors.

Subtraction specialists

Not all friction fixers tackle all problems. Zeroing in on one category of challenges can yield big results. The Friction Project focused particular attention on people who take responsibility for identifying, removing, and repairing what we call "jargon monoxide," the hollow, convoluted, and incomprehensible language that undermines workplace communication, collaboration, and coordination.

Take the team of seven workers from New Zealand's Nelson Hospital who replaced medical jargon with plain language in letters from physicians to patients. According to an article in *Internal Medicine Journal*, the team ran an experiment with 60 patients suffering from chronic health conditions. All 60 received the usual jargon-filled letter from a doctor that described their condition and suggested treatment, but the team randomly selected 30 patients to get a "translated" letter two weeks later—with common terms substituted for technical terminology. For example, "peripheral oedema" was translated into "ankle swelling," "tachycardia" into "fast heart rate," and "idiopathic" into "unknown cause."

Patients appreciated the clarity: Seventy-eight percent preferred the translated letter to the jargon-filled one, 69% said it had a positive impact on their relationship with their physician, and 80% reported that it increased their "ability to manage their chronic health condition." Patients were also asked to circle any terms in their letters that they didn't understand. Patients with untranslated letters circled eight terms, on average; those with translated letters circled two. The team's efforts to banish jargon monoxide eliminated unnecessary friction for patients.

Subtraction networks

Savvy friction fixers build, join, and activate networks to help them subtract obstacles. Civilla's leaders worked with numerous residents, community leaders, civil servants, and government officials during Project Re:form. Selzer told us that at first he made the mistake of stereotyping civil servants and officials as uncaring and unimaginative. But when he and fellow cofounders Michael Brennan and Lena Selzer started working with them, they found caring and conscientious people who despised that 42-page form—and were determined to fix it. Once those civil servants and officials realized that Civilla could help and had the wherewithal to stick with the problem, they served as supportive partners.

They helped the Civilla team navigate through hundreds of pages of government documents in order to develop a shorter and clearer form that still complied with regulations and laws. Civilla then worked with two offices of the MDHHS to test a prototype. After that successful pilot, Civilla helped train more than 5,000 field staffers in 100 department offices. The new form is 80% shorter than the old one, and the end-to-end processing time for frontline staffers has dropped by 42%—partly because they have 75% fewer errors to correct. Applications from residents have increased by 12%, yet because fewer need help completing them, lobby visits have dropped by 50%.

Subtraction movements

Sometimes efforts to reduce friction coalesce to become something greater than a series of activities—they become a movement. These enduring initiatives draw on the ideas and efforts of many people in an organization. Our case study on how pharmaceutical giant AstraZeneca scaled up simplicity is one example. It started when senior executives offered the senior director Pushkala Subramanian an intriguing job: to head an effort to simplify how the multinational's 60,000 employees worked. Subramanian couldn't resist the challenge, and in 2015 she launched the Simplification Center of Excellence. Her team was small, only four other employees, but their ambitions were big: The "million-hour challenge" aimed to give back 30 minutes a week to each employee in order to free up more time for clinical trials and serving patients.

Subramanian's team knew that a purely top-down approach would backfire because AstraZeneca is a decentralized company, where local leaders have substantial authority to accept, modify, or ignore orders from on high. So her team took a two-pronged approach. They made some companywide changes. In many parts of AstraZeneca, for example, it took days for new employees to get their company laptops. Subramanian's team worked with HR, hiring managers, and IT leaders to launch a program to ensure that every new employee had a functioning laptop and access to technical support on day one. Her team also led an effort that saved thousands of hours: changing the default meeting length on Outlook software from 30 minutes to 15 minutes.

At the same time, Subramanian's team waged a campaign to entice employees throughout the firm to make changes in their jobs, teams, and units. These efforts included identifying and recruiting "simplification champions" in major units who volunteered to lead local, grassroots changes. The simplification team provided websites, workshops, and coaches to help champions and other employees identify obstacles that frustrated them and their customers and supplied tools to help them implement local repairs.

In Brazil, for example, the simplification champion Roberto Uemura ran a two-week "waste hunters" contest that garnered 52 suggestions. One winning idea entailed streamlining a complex form and redesigning the system so that employees could more efficiently input information concerning patient safety issues from calls received through their unit's 1-800 number into a single database, rather than into different systems for transmission to headquarters, the local health agency, and other relevant parties. In Mexico the IT team cut paperwork in half, saving 690 hours a year. Meeting-free days were introduced in Taiwan and Thailand. Each employee in Japan simplified one thing, saving a collective 50,000 hours a year.

On May 17, 2017, AstraZeneca held World Simplification Day to celebrate saving two million hours in less than two years (twice the original goal!) and to spread time-saving practices throughout the company.

Bad friction is a plague that undermines productivity and creativity, raises costs, and frustrates employees, customers, and other stakeholders. It happens in large part because we default to asking, "What can I add here?" instead of "What can I get rid of?" But this penchant can be reversed by leaders who keep talking about and doing subtraction, teaching people how to practice it, and heaping kudos, cash, and other goodies on coworkers who remove unnecessary stuff.

Originally published in January–February 2024. **Reprint** R2401G

Where Does DEI Go from Here?

by Laura Morgan Roberts

IN THE SUMMER OF 2020, SPURRED BY the Black Lives Matter movement and pandemic inequities, organizations in the United States and around the world committed to improving diversity, equity, and inclusion (DEI) in their ranks. Today, however, amid economic uncertainty, corporate belt-tightening, and virulent campaigns to dismantle diversity efforts through both court rulings and legislation, the push for DEI has slowed. Now more than ever, it's time for companies to recommit.

To bring advocates and critics of this work together, leaders must orient around a broader goal: creating the conditions for all workers to flourish. Data on employee engagement underscores this challenge for organizations. Gallup estimates that 77% of employees are unengaged at work and reports that worker stress is at a historic high, costing the global economy $8.8 trillion. Union organizing across U.S. industries is highlighting the fact that many workers feel exploited or undervalued. Tens of millions of employees in the United States and more around the world switched jobs in the Great Resignation, and many others are quiet quitting or burning out. These kinds of trends lead to higher hiring costs and poorer performance, specifically diminished creativity and innovation. And there is evidence that those in historically marginalized groups are even less engaged than their dominant-group counterparts are.

In the past, corporate attempts to boost employee well-being have ranged from ping-pong tables to job crafting. But employers need to take a new tack that addresses the root of so many issues facing workers today. My research in the fields of positive psychology and diversity and inclusion leads me to believe that to truly engage each and every employee, and to help them feel validated and rewarded, organizations need to cultivate four freedoms that allow people to bring their full humanity to work.

The four freedoms that generate flourishing at work are: being our authentic selves, becoming our best selves, occasionally fading into the background, and failing in ways that help us and our teams learn. While everyone can benefit from more freedom at work, these four are unevenly distributed. Majority and high-status group members often (though not always) have access to them and often (though not always) take them for granted. Meanwhile, for many in traditionally marginalized groups—people of color, women, those who are gender nonconforming, people with physical disabilities, and those who are experiencing mental health challenges, for example—the struggle for liberation is contested daily.

To be sure, it can feel strange to talk about freedom in the context of the workplace, but it shouldn't. Around the world there is a history of forced labor, from the enslavement of humans on plantations to laborers in sweatshops, apartheid-era mines, or even Taylorist assembly lines. In many industries and parts of the world, people still work in such oppressive conditions. Even in the modern knowledge economy, employees struggle with fears—of failure, lack of safety, and scarcity of resources and opportunities—that undermine their feelings of freedom at work and negatively impact their performance and well-being.

By contrast, companies that have worked to make the four freedoms accessible—through structural changes such as policies and resource allocation, cultural shifts, and individual development—have seen enhanced productivity and increased feelings of satisfaction and safety among employees, particularly those in historically marginalized groups.

Idea in Brief

The Problem

Amid economic uncertainty, corporate belt-tightening, and efforts to dismantle diversity efforts through both court rulings and legislation, the push for diversity, equity, and inclusion has slowed. Given the high rates of disengagement and burnout, especially for those in historically marginalized groups, companies need a new approach.

The Path Forward

To bring advocates and critics of diversity together, leaders must orient around a broader goal: creating the conditions for all workers to flourish. Organizations must foster four freedoms at work: the freedom to be, the freedom to become, the freedom to fade, and the freedom to fail. Currently the four are unevenly distributed, but interventions such as encouraging individual allyship, implementing strengths-based development programs, and enabling flexible work can make organizations safer and more welcoming for all.

The fact is, liberating workers is not a zero-sum game; granting freedoms to one group does not inherently take them away from another. The collective pursuit of the four freedoms thus benefits everyone, as well as the business itself.

The Freedom to Be

We all flourish when we are granted the freedom to be our authentic selves at work. Consider, for example, the affirmation many people felt from colleagues when getting to know one another's pets and families through video calls during pandemic lockdowns. Being oneself at work may sound simple, but people who have the most affinity with the dominant culture often benefit from similarity and take this freedom for granted.

Those in historically marginalized groups, however, often lack that freedom and must expend significant effort on calibrating their authentic selves to fit into their surroundings. For example, racial minority group members often "whiten" their names on job applications by replacing ethnic-sounding names with initials or shortened

The Four Freedoms

THERE ARE FOUR FREEDOMS THAT HELP PEOPLE flourish at work. Majority and high-status group members often have more access to them than those in traditionally marginalized groups. Here are some ways that organizations can work to make sure that the four freedoms are realized by all.

Freedom to Be
The ability to bring our full, authentic selves to the workplace.

- **Nondiscrimination policies.** Know, meet, and, ultimately, surpass anti-discrimination policies set forth by law.

- **Antibias training.** Establish programs to overcome biases in hiring, promotion, and work opportunities as well as day-to-day interactions.

- **Allyship.** Encourage allyship through education and relationship building, both within and across identity groups.

Freedom to Become
The ability to improve our best selves and our situations.

- **Strengths-based development programs.** Overcome the praise deficits often faced by marginalized groups by offering development programs that recognize and focus on people's strengths.

nicknames; research has shown that this can improve their chances of a callback. Pregnant women hide their status to avoid stigmas and penalties. Other people avoid disclosing their parental status, sexual orientation, socioeconomic background, religion, or mental health issues. The latter is acute, for example, in Singapore, where surveys suggest that 62% of employees say they are unwilling to share their mental health challenges with colleagues or managers. Other employees might modify their speech or appearance to fit into their workplaces, such as by speaking a different vernacular language than they would at home or straightening their hair to fit the dominant model of professionalism.

These adjustments come with a cost. Research into code-switching and other forms of identity suppression has revealed the negative cognitive, health, and performance effects of maintaining a facade of conformity, as well as the feelings of inauthenticity it

- **Better feedback.** Coach and equip managers to give more positive, objective, constructive feedback to all.

Freedom to Fade

The ability to periodically step back from the spotlight and performance pressure.

- **Increased diversity.** Make heterogeneity the norm in the organization to take the spotlight off of members of traditionally underrepresented groups.

- **Flexible management.** Offer flexibility benefits, such as the ability to choose one's own schedule, and encourage managers to trust employees to calibrate or pull back on the days they need to.

Freedom to Fail

The opportunity for a second chance after a mistake.

- **Psychological safety.** Establish a culture in which failure is destigmatized and smart risks are rewarded.

- **Inclusion efforts.** Apply antidiscrimination and antibias efforts to the idea of failure to ensure that no one gets unfairly punished for falling short.

engenders. Patricia Hewlin of McGill University finds that inauthenticity can also cause direct problems for the organization: Employees who don't believe their true selves are valued tend to withhold dissenting thoughts and views, meaning they are less likely to speak up about perceived problems.

Granting everyone in the organization the freedom to bring their authentic selves to work takes continued efforts to establish and uphold nondiscrimination policies, antibias programming, and allyship.

Nondiscrimination policies

Organizations should know, meet, and, ultimately, surpass antidiscrimination policies set forth by law. For example, when companies' policies adhere to legislation like the CROWN Act (first enacted in California and now on the books in 23 U.S. states and

49 municipalities), which protects workers against race-based hair discrimination, they actively welcome a diverse range of employees to authentically express their racial identities. When they comply with the Respect for Marriage Act in the U.S. or the constitutional provision against sexual-orientation-based discrimination in Portugal, or go even further by providing health benefits to same-sex couples, they support employees of all sexual orientations. As workplaces become increasingly diverse, leaders will need to revisit internal policies in order to advance inclusion for a wider range of employee needs and lifestyles. Notably, dress codes are evolving to be more gender-neutral as well as more casual, aligning with both nondiscrimination legislation and postpandemic trends.

Antibias and inclusion programming
Beyond structural policies, programs aimed at overcoming biases in hiring, promotion, work opportunities, and day-to-day interactions can help more employees feel welcomed for who they are. These programs could include trainings for employees and managers to recognize and tackle their own biases; the establishment of clear, objective performance measures to use across the firm; and standardized questions for new-hire interviews. Of course, one-off trainings have limited impact on individual behavior or organizational culture, but when incorporated into broader, strategic approaches to DEI, they can add value.

Allyship
On an interpersonal level, allies—people who use their privilege to stand up for nondominant groups in the face of bias and ignorance—create an inviting and welcoming space for all. Their actions could include things as subtle as microvalidations, small gestures that can help to counteract the unwelcoming and disrespectful signals that microaggressions send. (Think of addressing people with their correct pronouns or titles, learning to pronounce someone's name, or expressing gratitude for a colleague's contributions.) Allyship also involves speaking out against discrimination, which can show up in ways as varied as pay inequity, sexual

harassment, or minority job applicants being rejected for a job without cause. Organizations can encourage allyship by establishing formal employee resource groups that provide opportunities for affinity-based learning, and by building personal connections across differences in people's multifaceted identities. They can also help managers and employees learn how to highlight people's strengths in order to counter discrimination.

MetLife is an organization known for its approach to inclusion globally, and specifically its efforts to promote employees' expression of their identities, values, and voice. The firm, where I've been hired to speak in the past, has established a number of policies that acknowledge and provide for professionals' whole selves, such as access to personalized caregiving solutions and Milk Stork transportation assistance for lactating mothers who need to ship expressed milk home during business travel. The company invites all employees to join or be an ally through its 10 identity-based inclusion networks (similar to employee resource groups). Firm-wide workshops, lectures, and podcasts remind MetLife employees that, as captured in the inclusion effort's tagline, "inclusion begins with me." Additionally, a cohort of 150 leaders in the firm were given coaching and tools to help them apply inclusive behaviors and habits to workplace interactions. The participants reported feeling more comfort with being their authentic selves, asking for help, and collaborating with colleagues. These efforts have paid off broadly in employee satisfaction: A 2022 survey, with the company's highest-ever response rate of 85%, reported record-high favorability ratings of 79%.

The Freedom to Become

Of course, we don't want to just be ourselves at work; we want our *best* selves to flourish. The freedom to *become* facilitates the practice of improving oneself and one's situation. The overwhelming majority of workers (91%) say it is very or somewhat important to them that their job consistently offers opportunities to learn and grow. Those who are satisfied with their opportunities for growth and development are much more likely to report being very or somewhat satisfied with their jobs (96%) than those who are not (64%).

Yet here, too, there is a historical precedent for a struggle for freedom: Caste, colonial, and socioeconomic systems have long locked individuals out of any form of social mobility. In today's workplace, for example, men are more likely to report being satisfied with growth and development opportunities (77%) than women are (71%), and people of color must wait longer to reach management and executive levels (if promoted at all) as a consequence of identity-based discrimination. Research by Joan Williams at the University of California College of the Law, San Francisco, and colleagues has shown that performance evaluations of Black and brown employees and white women have more mentions of failings than those of white men do. To address these inequities, organizations need to create development programs that play to everyone's strengths and make feedback processes more objective.

Strengths-based development programs

For all of us, living into our potential requires understanding where our potential and strengths lie. But research has shown that those in marginalized groups are exposed to a "praise deficit": Black and brown children receive far fewer compliments and more disciplinary action at school than their white peers do, for example. And research shows that this continues in the workplace. While managers regularly affirm the potential of early-career workers who belong to a majority group, they often subject workers from historically underrepresented groups to more scrutiny and give them less recognition for demonstrated success.

Companies need to establish high-quality development programs, accessible to all, that focus on what makes each employee their best. A more immediate and tactical way of addressing this issue is to integrate best-self exercises into employee development by inviting people to study their successes, exchange feedback about one another's strengths and contributions, and then discuss what they've learned. Mentorship and sponsorship programs also provide valuable ways to help all employees live into their potential—provided that they are offered in an equitable way. Much informal mentoring relies on networks that often are harder for people in marginalized groups to enter, so it is important to be intentional about helping everyone maximize their potential at work.

Positive, objective, constructive feedback

Organizations need to train managers to give more-constructive, more-objective feedback to everyone. Leadership development advisers Jack Zenger and Joseph Folkman have reported that 40% of managers say giving negative feedback is difficult and 37% avoid giving positive feedback altogether. Marcus Buckingham of the ADP Research Institute has described how managers tend to focus on deficits when giving feedback and shown why this impedes learning.

Those in marginalized groups are often given even less helpful performance feedback than those in dominant groups. For example, women don't receive the same quality of feedback as men; it tends to be vaguer, more aligned with feminine stereotypes, and more personality-based (even for positive feedback) and doesn't lead to advancement opportunities.

Research by Williams and colleagues shows that simply telling managers about common biases on performance evaluations lowers the incidence of those biases on future evaluations. And like many of the struggles for freedom described in this article, the effort to improve feedback and growth is well served by traditional efforts around DEI. People who work for an organization with DEI policies are more likely to report being satisfied with opportunities for growth and development (78%) than those in organizations without such policies (64%).

At TJX, owner of retail brands such as T.J.Maxx and Marshalls, the organization's Be Your Best Self learning platform gives associates courses, tools, and managerial support to empower them to build new skills and shape their career paths. The curriculum is designed to make consistent development accessible to all associates and includes partner offerings through organizations such as the National Hispanic Corporate Council, PFLAG, the National Association of Asian American Professionals, and the Human Rights Campaign. Recently, the company has added an online course on performance reviews that teaches managers to be more objective in the evaluation process. The company also offers an Emerging Leader program and has begun a mentorship pilot that pairs associates and leaders. Moreover, the TJX University program offers a coaching and mentoring approach to learning leadership skills.

These efforts contribute to some of TJX's diversity successes. In 2022, 35% of its managerial positions in the U.S. were held by people of color (versus 7% in other U.S. companies), 49% of its promotions in the U.S. were earned by people of color, and 68% of its managerial positions globally were held by women. One Marshalls employee, Afifah, began as a dressing room associate soon after emigrating to the U.S. from Pakistan. She quickly took on roles with increasing responsibility, using TJX's learning offerings to rise to a store manager role and then join the HR team. "At TJX," she explained, "I had many people tell me, 'You can do this.' They encouraged me and helped me grow along the way."

The Freedom to Fade

While the first two freedoms are about gaining the ability to stand out, the third freedom is all about being able to step back. In a dominant culture of hustle and perfectionism, employees need a way to take a break from the performance pressure.

For those in marginalized groups, diversity often yields a hypervisibility that means they are judged more harshly for perceived failures or deviations from the norm. Being an "only"—the only woman, the only person of Asian descent—in a room, on a team, or in an organization puts a person under increased scrutiny. This spotlight leaves individuals feeling vulnerable and exposed, with psychological ramifications such as perfectionism, reduced agency, higher disengagement, and obstructed career advancement. By contrast, increasing diversity and flexibility can help to foster freedom at work.

Increased diversity

Those in marginalized groups need the freedom to fade into the background or to blend in to escape scrutiny (as those in the dominant group often can). But they need to be able to do so in a way that doesn't require assimilation—losing what is unique and authentic about them—or invisibility—rendering their successes unseen and undermining their freedom to become. When heterogeneity becomes the norm in organizations—when being an only is rare—people feel more included and less scrutinized for their identities. Increasing diversity through focused hiring and development programs can help, especially at managerial and senior executive levels.

Flexible work

On a day-to-day basis, organizations can offer more flexibility benefits like choosing one's schedule, working in remote or hybrid arrangements, or being able to dedicate time to passion projects at work to allow for job crafting. For many hypercompetitive organizations, this is a full-scale culture change from the technology-enhanced, 24/7, always-accessible employment model. Some companies are encouraging this change by offering a four-day work-week, an approach that saw great success in a trial of 61 companies in Britain last year. Whatever the organization's policies, managers should treat all employees with dignity and respect by allowing them to manage their own energy and schedules. Flexible work also signals that employers trust people to fulfill their commitments even when they are working at different hours and in different locations.

Take Etsy, for example. The online sales platform for handmade and vintage items offers its employees a comprehensive work-life balance program that features unlimited sick and mental health days, sabbatical leave, and parental leave regardless of gender. It also takes a flexible approach to location, giving employees the options of working remotely full-time, working in the office, or adopting a flex schedule in which they're in the office a few days a month. Etsy's companywide "rest and recharge" days supplement its paid-time-off policies; mental health days and leaves reduce the stigma of disability and mental health. Finally, the company has

73

designated Focus Days, when noncritical meetings are canceled to help people do deep work.

These efforts are paying off: Etsy had the highest improvement ranking for employee engagement on the *Wall Street Journal*'s list of 250 top firms in 2022 and received a score of 92% on "Great place to work."

The Freedom to Fail

This freedom is the most important of all, because pursuit of all the other freedoms involves some degree of risk, and risk often leads, in the short term, to failure. When people know they'll be given chances to recover if they fail, it can help everyone embrace those freedoms with greater confidence.

This idea is borne out most famously in Harvard Business School professor Amy Edmondson's work on psychological safety in teams, which she defines as "a belief that one will not be punished or humiliated for speaking up with ideas, questions, concerns, or mistakes, and that the team is safe for interpersonal risk-taking." Other research confirms that people are able to thrive and flourish in contexts in which failure is met with a measure of agility and grace. (This doesn't mean they aren't held accountable for falling short; they still have to show they learned from the failure.) We also know that when work processes and people development systems are built to encourage psychological safety and learning from mistakes, employees and the organization benefit.

Many companies have worked to reduce the stigma around failure and, as Edmondson advocates, to develop a culture that supports taking smart risks by replacing shame and blame with curiosity, vulnerability, and personal growth.

But while these efforts are admirable and worthwhile, their benefits are not yet available to everyone. Members of the dominant group tend to have more second-chance opportunities, while across the globe those in marginalized groups are particularly vulnerable to being punished harshly for mistakes in the workplace, especially ones seen as a confirmation of negative stereotypes. For example,

Ashleigh Rosette of Duke University's Fuqua School of Business has found in several studies that Black leaders experience less generous interpretations of and more severe penalties for personal, team, and organizational failures than their counterparts do.

In order to grow, people need the freedom to fall short and try again in service of learning. Many of the antibias efforts and nondiscrimination policies described earlier in this article can play a role in diminishing the punishment gap between majority and minority groups, as can cultivating a culture that views everyone's mistakes as learning opportunities.

Organizations such as Google have been lauded for striving to increase psychological safety by encouraging bonding among team members, normalizing opportunities to learn from mistakes, and seeking input with humility and openness. Very few, though, have gone the extra mile to provide "second chances" in ways that increase access to opportunity and address systemic inequality. For people who have faced long-standing barriers to education and employment due to life circumstances or personal transgressions, the freedom to engage in gainful employment with dignity and fair wages is difficult to attain.

Kelly Services, a job placement firm, has built one pillar of its business around this idea. The firm connects employers hungry for talent and qualified people looking for work, especially in underrepresented groups such as neurodiverse talent, veterans, early- and late-career talent, women, and second-chance talent. The Kelly 33 Second Chances program, for example, focuses on the 78 million American adults who have a criminal history, which often disqualifies them from being able to find employment— even if they have only a nonviolent or minor drug offense on their record. The program has placed 645 people at Toyota, which reports that not one has been terminated for behavior correlated to their criminal history.

Kelly 33 is an example of how offering good jobs to those who need them most can have liberating effects on the workers and make a difference in society. For David Shaffer, one beneficiary of the program, being hired after many rejections because of his criminal record changed his whole perspective: "I was ready for another no, then I got a phone call . . . Now when I look at things, nothing's off limits for me anymore." Today Shaffer is a site manager who oversees 750 people.

———————

While I am advocating for worker liberation, I am not advocating for an anarchical approach to management in which employers have no responsibility or guardrails whatsoever, or in which employees do whatever they want without regard to anyone else. Author Toni Morrison reminds us that recklessness is not freedom, and that "the function of freedom is to free someone else." And in the words of author Audre Lorde, "Without community, there is no liberation."

The majority of workers recognize that the implicit agreement between employees and their employers is built on the compromise of freedom within constraints. I am simply advocating that this agreement be fair and just—and equally accessible to workers from all backgrounds and social categories. Employees don't want to feel that they must suppress who they are or put themselves in a box in order to succeed. They want to bring their real selves to work and pursue opportunities for growth that draw on their strengths. At the same time, they have to know that they can step back when necessary and that there is room for error as long as it helps them learn. When companies work toward the four freedoms, they align employees' core needs with their day-to-day work experiences, generating benefits for the individual as well as the organization.

Originally published on hbr.org, September 14, 2023. Reprint H07SLH

What Today's Rainmakers Do Differently

by Matthew Dixon, Ted McKenna, Rory Channer, and Karen Freeman

THE SELF-EVALUATION MEMO is an annual ritual at global law firm Baker McKenzie. At most firms, year-end self-appraisals consist of fee earners' perspectives on their own performance, but Baker McKenzie does things differently. It asks its partners to not just report on their own accomplishments but also point to specific instances in which they've successfully collaborated with colleagues—by, for example, introducing other partners with different areas of expertise to their clients. The firm expects its partners to expose clients to its broad array of services and to build new relationships—and in the process increase revenue. "Collaboration is crucial for Baker McKenzie," says Colin Murray, the firm's North America chief executive officer.

Because the partners know they will be asked to provide examples of collaboration in their year-end memos, they have an incentive to work with other lawyers across the firm throughout the year. Since switching to a collaborative approach six years ago, Baker North America has increased its revenue more than 40%.

Much research has been conducted to determine what makes top salespeople at B2B companies perform better than their peers. (See, for example, "The End of Solution Sales," HBR, July–August 2012.)

But little has been done on professional services firms, which have a unique go-to-market model in the B2B landscape. At most B2B companies, demand generation, sales, product delivery, customer success, and account management are discrete functions and tasks. But at professional services firms, partners are responsible for doing all of them. While most professional services firms have business-development support teams, the partners are "doer-sellers" and own the entire business-development and service-delivery life cycle. As "rainmakers," they must build awareness of their expertise in the market to generate demand, identify and close new client business, deliver the work, and then renew and expand the relationship over time.

For partners, becoming an effective business developer has long revolved around a central tenet: If you do good work and develop a strong relationship with your clients, they will come back to you the next time a need arises. But there is a growing problem with this belief—one that is rarely discussed openly. Clients—even long-standing ones for whom firms have delivered unquestioned value—are much less loyal than they once were. A survey we conducted of roughly 100 C-level executives revealed that as recently as five years ago, 76% of buyers preferred to buy again from partners or firms they had used in the past. Today, that figure is down to 53%—and over the next five years, it is expected to drop to 37%. So-called soft-spend categories such as management consulting, legal services, accounting, investment banking, PR, and executive search—once shielded by senior executives from formal procurement scrutiny—are now much more likely to be vetted as carefully as other spend categories. The result is that buyers are no longer defaulting to established relationships with premium-priced providers and now consider a range of alternative service providers, midtier players, and boutique firms. For their part, professional services firms report an increase in RFP-driven purchasing, a slowdown in repeat business from key clients, and pressure on rates, billable hours, and advisory fees. In this environment, the widening gap between high performers' and core performers' ability to bring in business is troubling and has increased the urgency to understand what the best rainmakers do differently.

Idea in Brief

The Problem

Business development at professional services firms has long revolved around one tenet: If you do good work for clients, they will keep coming back.

The Cause

But clients are no longer defaulting to established relationships with premium-priced providers and now often ask a range of service providers to compete for business.

The Solution

Three behaviors are core to a successful business-development approach: building connected networks of colleagues and clients, creating value through collaboration, and committing to a proactive and consistent business-development routine.

In collaboration with Intapp, a cloud software provider to professional services firms and a sponsor of the research, our team conducted a global study of nearly 1,800 partners from across 23 firms to identify how they approach business development. The in-depth survey collected data on partners' business-development preferences, behaviors, time allocation, and use of firm resources. In all, we evaluated more than 108 attributes for their impact on performance.

We also asked firm leaders to rate partners' business-development performance using a standard five-dimension scale. We then performed two types of statistical analysis on the data: regression (which looks at the impact of discrete variables on performance) and factor analysis (which looks at how variables group together into different business-development approaches). Our model included control variables to ensure that the findings were generalizable across the professional services industry. In addition, we conducted hour-long behavioral interviews with more than 80 top performers from across our sample population and 40 C-level executives from participating firms' client bases.

Our analysis revealed five distinct profiles that define how professional services partners approach business development. Overall, the profiles are equally represented across the firms we studied, but their relative performance is anything but equal. We found that four of the five (representing 78% of the partners in our study) are negatively correlated with performance. Only one—the Activator—shows a positive impact on performance and revenue. The Activator approach consists of three key behaviors: committing to business development, connecting with clients and colleagues, and creating value through collaboration.

In this article, we examine what makes the Activator approach so effective for professional services firms. We then detail the key characteristics of Activators and provide guidance on what firms can do to help every partner become an Activator.

The Five Business-Development Profiles

In accordance with decades of management guidance, professional services firms typically direct partners to pursue the appealing but ambiguous objective of building a competitive "moat" around their clients, which boxes out rivals and keeps clients coming back again and again. But rather than prescribing a preferred approach for doing so, firms tend to make business development a "choose your own adventure" for their client-facing partners. That's perhaps why we find the relatively even distribution of profiles across the professional services industry; at no firm do a majority of partners pursue the same approach. And while most of the partners in our study exhibited characteristics of more than one profile, each had a dominant one. Let's look at each profile in detail.

- *Experts* are best described as reluctant business developers. They focus on burnishing their public reputations as deep subject-matter experts—often through publishing, speaking, thought leadership, and so on—and assume that clients will seek them out for their services. Their business development consists primarily of responding to inbound demand from clients whose needs match their skill set and who already have a budget set aside. Much of their work comes from requests for proposals and competitive pursuits or from providing expertise on other partners' projects.

The Profiles at a Glance

FIVE DISTINCTIVE PROFILES characterize partners at professional services firms. Although an individual may exhibit traits from several different profiles, one will be dominant.

Expert

- Responds to established demand instead of proactively creating demand
- Leads with deep subject-matter expertise that matches client needs
- Prioritizes clients with established budgets

Confidant

- Is highly responsive to client needs
- Delivers exceptional service
- Builds deep relationships with clients
- Leverages strong track record of client work to get new business
- Emphasizes senior-most relationships

Debater

- Is very opinionated
- Loves to debate clients on what's best for their business
- Brings innovative solutions to the client
- Expects the client to agree with the plan of action

Realist

- Focuses on setting proper expectations with the client
- Openly discusses budgets, fees, and schedule issues with the client
- Is comfortable telling the customer no
- Deliberately avoids no-win situations

Activator

- Leverages events and social platforms to build a robust client network
- Educates clients on critical trends and issues
- Proactively engages clients on new opportunities to work together
- Introduces clients to other partners and practice areas

- *Confidants* are extremely client-centric, highly responsive, and focused on building a reputation for executing superior work. These partners rely on relationships with clients that date back to law school, business school, or previous jobs. Because of how much they've invested in building the relationships, they are quite protective of them internally. And having established a track record of excellent work, they expect clients to return to them automatically. Of all the partner profiles we identified, Confidants are closest to the classic "trusted adviser" model that is often held up as the gold standard in the industry.

- *Debaters* are contrarians who have strong opinions about how projects should be executed and are unafraid to share them, often pushing clients outside their comfort zones. They believe they know best and expect clients to follow their lead. Curiously, this posture is one that we've found in previous work to be highly correlated with strong performance in B2B sales. However, the relative underperformance of Debaters in professional services suggests that while this profile may be effective when selling products like software, it falls short when the person doing the selling *is* the product. As one C-level client told us, "I want the partners I work with to push my thinking. But if every time we sit down I'm being told I'm 'doing it wrong,' it just becomes mentally exhausting."

- *Realists* pride themselves on their transparency and honesty with clients. In our survey of C-level buyers, only 10% of respondents said that their trust in partners and firms has increased over the past five years. In a market crowded with partners who overstate their experience and capabilities and frustrate clients with outsize invoices, Realists are completely transparent about what they can and can't deliver, what services will cost, and what the client should realistically expect in terms of outcomes and value. As such, they aim to avoid putting themselves in "no win" situations—for example, engagements that are unlikely to produce their intended results or work that can't be delivered on time or on budget.

This approach is very effective in completing work that meets expectations, but Realists' "glass half empty" attitude can be off-putting for clients who prefer an aspirational approach.

- *Activators* are network builders. They spend a significant portion of their business-development time identifying and engaging with prospective clients through tools such as LinkedIn and at industry and firm-sponsored events. Activators focus on establishing relationships across client functions

How the profiles affect performance

This chart illustrates the effect on revenue when the average-performing partner leans harder into a particular profile. Moving from a weak to a strong demonstration of Activator skills results in a revenue-generation increase of up to 32%. The opposite is true for the other approaches, all of which are negatively correlated with performance. For example, a shift from weak to strong in the Expert profile results in a drop in revenue generation of up to 15%.

Performance impact (revenue generation)

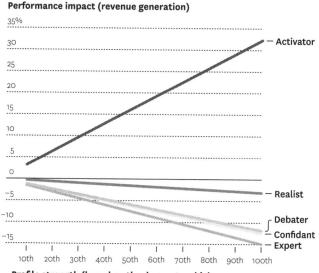

Profile strength (based on the degree to which a person demonstrates the attributes associated with a given profile)

and up and down the org chart. Their business-development approach tends to be proactive. They "harvest" business from their network—for example, reaching out to current and prospective clients when changes occur in the regulatory or economic environment. They also look for opportunities to introduce their clients to partners from other practice areas in their firm who they think can provide value. In our regression and analysis, the professionals who most strongly exhibited the behaviors that typify the Activator pattern had the most positive impact on revenue. (See the exhibit "How the profiles affect performance.")

The Activator Playbook

The Activator profile is characterized in large part by three key behaviors.

Committing to business development as a crucial part of the job

Activators understand that providing excellent service does not guarantee the next piece of work, so they carve out and protect time for business development. And they balance their efforts between growing existing client relationships and adding new clients to their roster.

Because partners in professional services firms are responsible for not just selling but also delivering the work, business development often gets crowded out by other tasks, especially when a partner doesn't have a natural bent toward it. Non-Activators spend 37% less time on business development than Activators do and report that they do business development only when time allows. Nearly 90% of Activators report that they reserve time for business development every week; only one-third of partners with other profiles report the same. And Activators balance client-facing business-development time in roughly equal portions between new and existing clients (22% new and 23% existing), whereas non-Activators, consistent with their belief that performing good work for clients will automatically lead to the next piece of business, dedicate nearly twice as much time to existing clients as to potential clients (32% existing and 17% new).

Adam Ludwiczak, a partner at Marathon Capital, a financial services firm with a focus on renewable energy projects, told us that he maps out his business-development activities before the workweek begins. Every Sunday night, he writes three categories on a blank sheet of paper: client interactions, deal-specific action items, ways to engage prospects and clients. As he plans the week's business-development time, he uses that framework as a guide for whom to reach out to and for what reason. At the end of each day, he emails notes to his direct reports, who feed them into Marathon's CRM system. He tags relevant parties on opportunities so that team members can work together to keep the business-development pipeline moving.

Katie Vickery, a partner at the UK law firm Osborne Clarke, has a commitment to her business-development routine that has paid off handsomely. She told us that she spends half of every workday on business development. She posts on LinkedIn, likes or comments on others' posts, and keeps track of role changes and personal events. She reads as much as possible, scanning the news in search of valuable updates that she can send to clients. She also creates thought leadership videos: When inspiration strikes, she goes into Osborne Clarke's in-house studio, records a video in about 20 minutes, and posts it on LinkedIn. Her process nets her roughly one new business opportunity every two to three days.

Connecting with prospects, clients, and colleagues

Activators build robust networks of current and prospective clients, subject-matter experts, and others who can provide value. They use their networks to surface new business opportunities, turning contacts into clients. Activators do this not just for themselves but for their colleagues, connecting clients and prospects with other partners and practice areas within their firms.

Activators also build networks across client organizations rather than cultivate relationships only with top senior decision-makers. They operate under the assumption that no client relationship is

What Activators Do Well

THESE BUSINESS-DEVELOPMENT BEHAVIORS can help you improve your performance.

Commit

- Reserve time to conduct business development every week
- Protect time for business development from being crowded out by other work
- Consistently engage with clients and prospects
- Rigorously follow up on opportunities that have been discussed
- Track contacts and follow-ups in your firm's CRM system

Connect

- Make a significant number of LinkedIn connections
- Make a concerted effort to expand the number of contacts in your network
- Regularly check and post on LinkedIn
- Regularly attend business events
- Set specific goals for post-event calls or meetings
- Look for opportunities to connect clients with colleagues who can provide value

Create

- Regularly reach out to clients with updates on regulatory, economic, or other trends
- Proactively identify new ways to work with clients
- Check in regularly to assess clients' current needs
- Provide advice to clients and prospects even when you are not actively engaged in paid work

"safe" and understand that senior executives are less likely than they were in the past to "put their thumb on the scale" for current professional services partners despite long-standing business and personal relationships. So they develop connections with team members across the client organization who, though they may not hold the purse strings, have influence over how decisions are made.

Non-Activators tend to focus narrowly on a small handful of key clients. They spend far less time on platforms like LinkedIn and are less purposeful in their use of firm events. A common behavior (particularly with Confidants and Experts) is to hoard their relationships and avoid introducing clients to colleagues in their firm. Client relationships are a zero-sum game for them: Bringing in a colleague would divert the client's attention away from them as the sole source of value. Worse, the colleague could destroy the hard-earned relationship by, for example, providing poor service. Only 29% of non-Activators frequently introduce clients to other colleagues in their firms—compared with 73% for Activators, who sell the collective "we" of their firms rather than just the "me" of their personal expertise.

Tom Day, a partner at PA Consulting, took that approach with his team to create opportunities with a potential client at a consumer-packaged-goods (CPG) firm. Tom's team realized that its CEO was active on LinkedIn and started responding to his posts. One day, the CEO liked a reply from one of the team members. In a follow-up post, the team invited the CEO to visit PA Consulting's R&D lab. The CPG company's head of innovation began following the thread; then she liked another post, and her team reached out to Tom's to set up a visit to the lab. Thanks in part to those connections, the CPG firm engaged PA Consulting for a seven-figure deal, as well as two other large projects. "It's about getting to the right people inside a monster of an organization," he says. Had he pinged the CEO directly without help from his team, the effort would have likely gone unnoticed.

Kelly Kay, the global managing partner of the software practice at executive search firm Heidrick & Struggles, also believes in the value of connecting clients with other colleagues across the firm. For instance, if he's speaking with a CEO who is considering forming an international leadership team, he will make an introduction to his international colleagues. Partners in many other firms don't do this because they don't trust one another or because their compensation plan doesn't incentivize the behavior. But Heidrick & Struggles encourages and rewards this kind of collaboration within the firm. Kelly says this philosophy has led to significant new business for Heidrick as well as for himself and his colleagues.

Searching for ways to create value

Activators help current and prospective clients by curating information (about regulatory changes, court rulings, economic indicators, news events, and so on) that they need to be aware of. Activators then proactively engage clients in conversations about potential issues and opportunities.

Even if opportunities for creating value fall outside their area of expertise, Activators do not shy away from engaging their clients. If they aren't best positioned to provide services, they connect clients with other partners in their firm or subject-matter experts within their networks. They work hard to avoid situations in which the client has already identified a need and is asking firms to compete for the business. Instead, Activators are forward-looking. They realize that even if some of this outreach doesn't translate into billable work in the short term, it lays the groundwork for engagements down the road.

Most partners strive to be highly responsive to client needs, which in business-development terms often means that they are reactive—typically waiting until a need is expressed before having a commercial conversation. Fully 73% of Activators prefer to proactively engage clients with an opportunity, compared with just 36% of non-Activators.

Eric Tresh, a partner at the law firm Eversheds Sutherland (a client of ours), spends most mornings reviewing recent tax-court decisions. He then identifies clients and prospects in his network for which the rulings present an opportunity or a threat. He drafts messages to his connections in those organizations and proposes that they meet to discuss the implications. He understands that his clients don't have time to monitor the tax courts in all the jurisdictions in which they operate, so he does it for them. He doesn't do empty check-ins: He sends a message only if he truly thinks it's a relevant development. His clients tell him that when they hear from him, they know it isn't spam and that he's got something of value for them.

Building a Team of Activators

Driving change in professional services firms is unlike driving change in a typical B2B company, where a chief sales or revenue officer can lay out a strategy, dictate a sales process, and require reps to adhere to the playbook. At professional services firms, partners are co-owners of the business, and their expertise is the very product the firm is selling. As a result, partners are often free to do what they please when it comes to business development.

Firms looking to cultivate an Activator approach need to therefore pursue a "push-pull" strategy. They should nudge partners toward Activator behaviors while making the approach the path of least resistance. To do so, firms should make investments in four key areas:

Training and coaching

McDermott Will & Emery has a unique approach to business development, a key component of which is a global training program for partners on managing their networks. Over the past five years, the firm has trained over 500 partners, resulting in stronger client relationships and helping increase firm revenue. The firm has grown from $800 million to $1.8 billion, making it the fastest-growing law firm in the United States.

Eversheds Sutherland also provides business-development training for its fee earners. But unlike most firms, Eversheds starts the program at the associate level, several years before these professionals are even considered for partner. The program is taught by the firm's business-development team, allowing associates to forge stronger, more value-added relationships with that team's members—relationships that will really pay off when the associates make partner.

Hiring and partner selection

Traditionally, firms have focused on technical expertise, client impact, and book of business as the criteria for making partner-selection and hiring decisions. But our research suggests that other criteria should be emphasized as well—for instance, a candidate's proclivity for collaboration. This is particularly important for firms that use the hiring of competitors as a growth lever. Bringing in Confidants or Experts from other firms—even if they are proven rainmakers—can be a costly mistake if they refuse to collaborate or can't cultivate an Activator mindset.

For firms with a deficit of Activators, a smart way to deploy this scarce talent (until others can be hired or trained to be Activators) is to assign them to be relationship managers on the firm's largest and highest-potential client opportunities—something that a number of progressive organizations, like law firm Faegre Drinker, strive to do. While the other four partner profiles have certain strengths and can add to the diversity and impact of a client-facing team, firms would be well-advised to make sure the person running point for their largest clients fits the Activator mold.

Technology

Firms can significantly boost Activator behaviors by investing in technology. Generative AI, such as ChatGPT and Google Bard, can help partners surface client-relevant insights from massive amounts of publicly available information. CRM systems can prompt partners to proactively engage clients at certain time intervals or when client-related issues arise. Social platforms like LinkedIn help partners identify prospects with whom they should be connected. Internal social-networking tools, such as Slack and

Microsoft Teams, help partners identify colleagues with whom they can collaborate.

Capstone Partners, one of the largest middle-market investment-banking firms in the United States, uses relationship intelligence software to reveal connections between partners and prospects. That firm uses the technology to apply relationship scores to colleagues, contacts, and clients, and based on that data it builds highly targeted buyer lists. This helps ensure effective outreach and streamlined communication between partners, clients, and prospects. The technology also enables bankers to quickly identify the right person to contact at each target company and to capture and track touchpoints and interactions with prospects, making lead-generation efforts more efficient.

Finnegan, a leading boutique intellectual-property law firm, leverages firmwide experience-management technology to capture deep insights into practices, industries, courts, judges, clients, court filings, and the varied technical experience of the firm's IP professionals. Using that catalog of the firm's collective work experience, technical expertise, and subject-matter profiles, partners can easily identify and spotlight the colleagues who bring the right skills, knowledge, and expertise to potential engagements, and thereby win more work from existing and new clients.

Incentives and rewards

Firms must reinforce the Activator behavior they wish to see replicated throughout the organization. Baker McKenzie's requirement that partners identify collaborations with colleagues as part of their compensation memos is one way to incentivize collaboration. McDermott Will & Emery encourages healthy competition among its partners by asking them to log at least two business-development activities a week. Qualifying activities are substantive in nature, such as attending a pitch meeting, networking with contacts at an event, and nonbillable sharing of insights or trends. Firm leaders recognize partners who demonstrate a steady commitment to developing business, and clients acknowledge the positive impact on their working relationships and support to their businesses.

In a world in which clients are less loyal to professional services firms and strong relationships are no guarantee of getting the next piece of business, Activators build robust networks of clients, prospects, and colleagues. By being proactive in their business-development approach, they are far more likely to create demand rather than end up facing off against the competition.

Originally published in November–December 2023. Reprint R2306D

The New Era of Industrial Policy Is Here

by Willy C. Shih

GOVERNMENTS AROUND THE WORLD are increasingly intervening in the private sector through industrial policies designed to help domestic sectors reach goals that markets alone are unlikely to achieve. As a result, companies in targeted sectors—such as automakers, energy companies, and semiconductor manufacturers—may experience dramatic changes in their operating environments. The policies could create new costs or deliver financial incentives to shift R&D or manufacturing investments. They may also incent firms to alter their supplier networks or change their trading partners. Managers who have grown up in markets without such interventions are now facing an unfamiliar environment. This article will provide an overview of policy approaches and give managers a framework for responding to them.

The Fall and Rise of Industrial Policy

Industrial policies are not new. Countries have long practiced them: Japan used *gyōsei shidō*, or "administrative guidance," coupled with loans, grants, subsidies, and other financial tools, after the Second World War to foster the growth of its manufacturing sector. In 1986 China launched its 863 program to modernize technology. South

Korea, Singapore, and Taiwan all used programs to stimulate modernization and development. In the United States the Apollo space program and the work of the Defense Advanced Research Projects Agency (DARPA) are examples of mission-oriented industrial policies that successfully stimulated innovation. Yet over the last few decades, critics have questioned whether such interventions were the most efficient way to allocate public resources. Failures to achieve objectives, perceived anticompetitive effects, concerns about crowding out private investments, and the view that programs often ended up serving special interests all fueled the skepticism. As did high-profile failures such as the U.S. investment in solar panel maker Solyndra, the Synthetic Fuels Corporation (established in 1980 and closed six years later), and the commercial failure of the British and French Concorde supersonic passenger jetliner. Consequently, the pendulum swung the other way; many governments intervened less.

During the past five years, the pendulum has been swinging quickly back, propelled in part by the need to respond to global societal challenges such as the Covid-19 crisis and climate change. In addition, many countries fear that their strategic technologies or sectors are weakening, which poses a threat to economic growth, national security, and innovation capacity. Some new industrial policies focus on creating jobs; others on influencing international trade. Notable examples include the European Green Deal, Horizon 2020, and the Strategic Forum for Important Projects of Common European Interest (IPCEI); the Infrastructure Investment and Jobs Act (IIJA), the Inflation Reduction Act (IRA), and the CHIPS and Science Act in the United States; and policies in China like Made in China 2025 and its Belt and Road Initiative, which some argue was designed to grow its export trading ecosystem.

Sometimes governments intervene because the private sector may not be willing to assume as much risk as governments when it comes to providing public goods. Operation Warp Speed in the United States is a case in point. It was highly successful in accelerating clinical trials and introducing new technologies like mRNA

Idea in Brief

The New World

A new age of industrial policy is at hand. Governments have been increasingly intervening in the private sector as they have struggled to cope with the pandemic, rising geopolitical tensions, evolving economies, and climate change.

The Challenges

For businesses, government policies are creating new costs and forcing them to rethink where they conduct research, make

products, and source components and materials.

The Solution

Business leaders should understand the competing interests shaping the policies, engage and educate political leaders and their staffs, collaborate with upstream and downstream partners, and weigh the pros and cons of accepting government incentives. They must adapt to the new rules of the game.

vaccines, diagnostics, and therapeutics to fight Covid-19 because the Biomedical Advanced Research and Development Authority (BARDA) was willing to absorb large financial risks by betting on a portfolio of different technologies, including ones that had never been deployed.

A more controversial, and increasingly common, type of intervention focuses on helping specific industries or sectors. European governments' support for Airbus helped the consortium overcome the high fixed costs of entering the commercial aircraft industry; China offered the same kind of support to the Commercial Aircraft Corporation of China (COMAC) to design and produce passenger jets such as the C919. China, which has long relied on industrial policies to develop its economy, also intervened heavily with subsidies in solid-state lighting, wind energy, and solar panel manufacturing. And recognizing early on the strategic importance of transitioning its automotive industry to electric, China also provided incentives to buyers of domestically made electric vehicles. The country became the world's largest manufacturer of electric vehicles, and Chinese companies such as Contemporary Amperex Technology Company (CATL) and BYD have become dominant suppliers of lithium batteries and their components. Such successes have encouraged governments everywhere to intervene more in technology-focused and mission-oriented industrial strategies.

The intensifying geopolitical competition between the United States and China is adding fuel to the fire. The U.S. government has tried to reverse the declines of strategic sectors in its manufacturing base by offering significant subsidies and loans, erecting tariffs, and providing extensive tax incentives coupled with domestic content rules, such as those provided in the Federal Advanced Manufacturing Production Tax Credit of the Inflation Reduction Act. It has issued new rules governing ownership of entities and export bans, such as those for advanced semiconductors and the equipment needed to make them. These policies have led to a big jump in manufacturing investment in the United States but have prompted other countries, including allies, to counter with their own interventions. The EU, for instance, responded with its Green Deal Industrial Plan and proposals to temporarily set aside state-aid rules that limited subsidies to companies in member countries. South Korea's parliament approved the K-Chips Act in response to the U.S.'s CHIPS and Science Act.

Industrial policies have also begun to spill across national or supranational borders (like the EU) with the emergence of new alliances and concepts like friend-shoring, or the sourcing of materials and components from trusted trade partners. Examples include the Chip 4 Alliance proposed by the Biden administration, which would create a "democratic semiconductor supply chain" that spans Japan, South Korea, Taiwan, and the United States; the Group of 7 agreement to collectively manage risks in critical mineral supply chains; and the UK–Japan semiconductor partnership.

Friend-shoring and industry-specific trade alliances add another challenge for companies that operate across borders: Executives need to understand not only the competitive dynamics of potentially unfamiliar markets in other countries but also the possible impacts of policy decisions in countries with competing sectors. For example, the United States has no flat-panel-display industry and relies on China, Japan, South Korea, and Taiwan for its entire supply of computer monitors, TVs, and displays used in cars and other equipment. But Chinese policies that resulted in overinvestment in manufacturing capacity will likely drive U.S. "friends" such as South Korea, Japan, and Taiwan out of the business, which will eventually force U.S. companies to source exclusively in China.

Navigating the Changing Policy Environment

As new policies are formulated and implemented, business leaders can take steps to position themselves wisely:

Recognize the different forms of industrial policy

Industrial policies fall into four broad categories: horizontal, vertical, supply-side, and demand-side. It is helpful for managers to recognize the distinctions because each impacts market behavior and competition differently.

Horizontal policies apply to all firms irrespective of their activities, their location, or the technologies they use. They include things like R&D tax credits and accelerated depreciation, which reduce the costs of capital investments. Vertical, or targeted, policies favor a specific sector or firm. They include renewable-energy tax credits like those provided for in the IRA: a $3 per kilogram credit for the manufacture of solar-grade polysilicon and a credit of $12 per square meter for making photovoltaic wafers.

Supply-side policies mainly impact the cost of R&D or production, and they can tilt the playing field in favor of certain locations or the use of particular materials or technologies. Governments use supply-side tools such as grants, subsidies, tax preferences, and tax credits most frequently. Economists argue that they may be justified when firms don't have sufficient incentives to invest in risky projects or they underinvest because they will get only a partial share of the total return on their investment. For example, the European Battery Alliance is channeling billion of euros into research and innovation, while in the United States the IRA provides credit subsidies and loan guarantees for a range of clean energy projects.

Demand-side tools, by contrast, typically affect domestic consumption of targeted products or services. They work to increase the size of the market overall. Examples include tax credits for the purchase of an electric vehicle and guaranteed pricing for renewable power sold to the operator of an electrical grid. Government procurement is another demand-side tool, as are tax credits for the installation of renewable-energy generation. Demand-side tools have the advantage of preserving market competition among companies vying to sell to customers, but nonetheless they distort markets, at least temporarily. Many provisions in the Inflation Reduction Act that support clean energy are essentially demand-side tools that contain domestic content rules.

Many companies focus on supply-side tools when they are lobbying because supply-side policies can be narrowly targeted to give their business an advantage. They expect that demand-side policies will create more competition for them. But lobbying for a combination of supply- and demand-side policies would often be more effective, as demand-side tools increase the size of the market, which creates more incentives for firms to invest—and lowers the risk of those investments.

Understand competing priorities and government intent

When policies are still being developed, it is important for executives to understand the multiple interests at play. For the CHIPS and Science Act, for instance, the government's highest priority was securing domestic sourcing of semiconductors for defense and critical infrastructure needs. Semiconductor makers, for their part, wanted help competing against lower-cost foreign competition; chip customers like automakers wanted a dependable supply; and organized labor wanted high-paying union jobs. Most policies are compromises that draw political support from a wide spectrum of constituencies.

Engage and educate

Before industrial policies are finalized, many organizations employ their government relations teams or lobbyists to try to shape them in ways that serve their interests. But executives often fail to appreciate the importance of educating not only political leaders and appointees but also career civil servants who write the legislation—such as congressional staffs in the United States or EU staff in Brussels. Many civil servants have minimal experience in the business world, and areas like green energy or semiconductors are technically complex. That gives CEOs a unique opportunity to offer meaningful input, especially when they can speak for an industry sector.

Focusing on educating government officials and staff members about competing interests and issues may be a more effective way to shape the thinking of the people developing the policies than simply advocating for a particular measure. It entails temporarily setting aside a firm's specific interests and conveying the big picture: the industry's structure, existing trade dynamics, and how all the pieces connect. For example, recent semiconductor trade policies were motivated by the supply chain crisis that arose during the Covid-19 pandemic, when multiple strategic vulnerabilities were exposed. Yet many people in government and business fell into the trap of looking only one step upstream or one step downstream from where shortages appeared, which led to intense and competing lobbying around potential solutions. Taking a bird's-eye view of the highly interconnected network of chip designers, materials suppliers, chip manufacturers, and chip consumers would have been a better approach. Then policy makers would have recognized that some bottlenecks in the supply chain were connected to demand surges and stockpiling in the face of looming U.S. sanctions on Chinese companies, and that automakers shared their call on chip foundry capacity with other sectors experiencing high demand. It would also have helped them understand how U.S. sanctions on select Chinese companies had triggered the construction of excessive capacity in mature chip sectors in China and was likely to result in commoditization pressure on other global players.

In a similar vein, many people in government may not appreciate how investment levels and time horizons for earning returns vary across sectors and even within a sector. Pharmaceutical companies and semiconductor companies might spend 30% or more of their revenue on R&D, whereas consumer goods companies might spend

2% or less. As a policy tool, tax credits are beneficial only when a firm has income to apply those credits against. Capital-intensive industries such as semiconductor manufacturing and mining may not turn a profit for 10 years or more. In such cases, offering a tradable credit would allow those companies to sell the tax preference to another business. For example, U.S. energy policy between 1918 and 1970 focused on increasing domestic oil and gas reserves. It offered the industry a host of incentives, including tax tools such as the expensing of intangible drilling and dry hole costs; a percentage-depletion allowance to counter the exhaustion of underground reserves; favorable treatment of capital gains on the sale of successful properties; and special exemptions from rules for limitations on passive activity losses. Taken together, they reduced the marginal tax rate in the oil and gas industries and helped put U.S. firms at the forefront of upstream production for most of the 20th century. But those approaches were formulated long before many of today's lawmakers were born. If corporate executives spend time educating them, they'll be more likely to formulate more-nuanced policies.

Collaborate
Working with upstream and downstream partners in your supply chain can lead to commercially successful outcomes that are aligned with industrial policy objectives. In Europe, many companies that are responding to mandates to reduce carbon emissions face a "chicken and egg" problem: Companies may hesitate to switch to a more sustainable fuel because sources of supply down the road are uncertain. At the same time, potential fuel suppliers cannot or will not invest in more capacity unless they are assured that there will be sufficient sustained demand to earn a return on their investment. A.P. Moller-Maersk, the Danish shipping and logistics giant, tried to address that dilemma by signing offtake agreements with biomethanol suppliers to get them to commit to investing in new production capacity. Similarly, General Motors is investing $650 million in Lithium Americas to help it develop its new Thacker Pass mine in Nevada, a deal that includes a 10-year offtake agreement and options to secure even more of the mine's output.

Adapt

The late Harvard Business School professor Bruce Scott described business as an activity conducted on a playing field that is operating under rules set by the government. From this perspective, new industrial policies are an attempt to change the rules of play in order to achieve specific goals.

Adaptability, therefore, is critical for business leaders. The RISC-V Foundation, an organization set up to foster the adoption of its open-source processor core technology (developed at the University of California, Berkeley), moved its headquarters from the United States to Switzerland, renaming itself RISC-V International in the process. It did so to ensure that its members, which include U.S., European, and Chinese companies, could continue to use RISC-V chip designs in the face of increasing trade restrictions.

Another example of adaption: Some Western companies that have large businesses in China are bifurcating their supply chains to serve the Chinese market separately from the rest of the world. And many Western firms that are dependent on China for most of their production needs but can't move to other countries yet will need to develop road maps to diversify their production over the long term.

Decide whether to accept subsidies

Demand-side subsidies are relatively straightforward. The seller's task is to comply with requirements that enable a buyer of its product to collect the subsidy. When government programs offer supply-side subsidies, however, business leaders must decide whether to accept them. U.S. programs increasingly have strings attached, ranging from the traditional, such as meeting minimum investment or hiring levels, to the nonconventional, such as the government taking equity stakes, financial stakes, or shares in future earnings. During Operation Warp Speed, for instance, Moderna's executives accepted funding from BARDA to accelerate development and scale up manufacturing. By contrast, Pfizer's leaders took a more limited approach: The company received a government commitment to purchase 100 million doses of its vaccine after it successfully manufactured it and received the Food and Drug Administration's emergency-use authorization. Both vaccines were commercially successful, but Moderna's closer collaboration with the government probably contributed to subsequent disputes between the company and the National Institutes of Health over patent ownership and which companies had the right to license the technology.

Subsidies can bring other constraints. An extreme case in point is the U.S. government's bailout of GM during the Great Recession. The 2008 financial crisis caused a precipitous drop in sales for domestic automakers, leaving them in financially precarious positions. Concerns about the collapse of a major industry prompted the federal government to step in. GM received more than $50 billion as part of the Troubled Asset Relief Program (TARP), but it had to grant 60.8% of shares in a New GM to the U.S. Treasury and the balance of shares to the United Auto Workers retiree health care trust fund, the governments of Canada and Ontario, and holders of the old GM's bonds. The Obama administration pressured GM's then-CEO Rick Wagoner to resign, and the company went through a restructuring directed by the administration's Auto Task Force, effectively ceding management control to the government.

Plan to live without subsidies or preferences in the long term

Once a firm accepts subsidies or tax preferences, managers need to plan for the time when that support ends. Construction subsidies offered under the CHIPS and Science Act, for example, will likely be onetime events, designed to help offset high construction costs. But these subsidies alone will not reduce operating costs except to the extent that they reduce the cost of capital and consequently lower amortization per wafer produced. Plus they come with strings attached—there may be restrictions on companies' ability to invest in other countries in the future or other constraints on their future operations. The ultimate question for executives will be how to address higher costs for materials (much of which will still need to be imported), availability of skilled workers, and other ancillary costs.

One theory behind subsidies in the IRA and CHIPS and Science Act is that manufacturers will build scale and lower their costs by moving down the learning curve, and that may be true. But it is important for businesses leaders to understand that government objectives are not necessarily focused on company profitability. For example, the CHIPS and Science Act has as its highest priority ensuring domestic access to advanced semiconductor manufacturing capacity for military and essential commercial uses. It is not designed to ensure the profitability of manufacturers' domestic operations. That's up to the companies' leadership. In a similar vein, some subsidies under the IRA or IIJA will require higher percentages of domestic content over time and will be phased out over time, so managers need a plan to be competitive when that happens.

We are moving into a new world order, where governments around the world are increasingly using industrial policy tools to shape where companies structure and locate their operations, which products they sell, and to whom they sell them. For companies that operate in multiple countries, navigating those policies won't be easy. Managers need to understand the goals of the governments, work to educate government officials and staff to shape policies as they are being developed, and figure out how to optimally revamp their operations accordingly. Corporate strategies built during what we will probably look back on as a golden age of globalization will have to be recast for a more fragmented world, taking into account different country contexts and constraints and tailoring approaches that fit these markets. It will be much harder to have one size fit all.

Originally published in September–October 2023. Reprint R2305D

How to Market Sustainable Products

by Frédéric Dalsace and Goutam Challagalla

WHEN COMPANIES MARKET the sustainability features of their offerings, they often overlook a fundamental truth: Social and environmental benefits have less impact on customers' decisions than basic product attributes do. With any purchase, consumers are first trying to get a specific job done. Only after they find something that will help them do that job—and only if sustainability is important to them—will they look for a product that in addition confers a social or environmental advantage. No one decides to buy a chocolate bar to, say, improve the working conditions of farmers on the Ivory Coast. People buy chocolate, first and foremost, because they want to indulge in a small pleasure. No one decides to buy an electric car to prevent climate change. People buy cars because they need transportation; reducing their carbon footprint is an ancillary benefit.

Missing this critical point, many marketers overestimate consumers' appetite for sustainable products. Because of that, in recent years companies have flooded the market with sustainable offerings that consumers are slow to buy, particularly given the price premium such products typically command. Though products that incorporate environmental or social messaging now account for 48% of new consumer packaged goods, their share of the overall U.S. consumer goods market remains relatively low. In 2021 it was only 17%, up from 14% in 2015, according to a report from New York University's Center for Sustainable Business. The misalignment between what companies offer and what consumers want is evident not just in B2C sectors but in B2B ones as well.

Drawing on an extensive three-year research initiative at IMD business school that encompassed surveys, interviews, and interactive sessions with more 500 executives in B2B and B2C sectors from various countries, we've created a guide for sustainability marketing that builds on a more nuanced understanding of how consumers weigh the relative value of traditional and social and environmental benefits. With clarity on how consumers make this calculation, executives can devise product and service strategies that will maximize their chances of success.

Balancing Benefits

Marketers often imagine that sustainability features simply layer additional value on top of an offering's traditional benefits. But in reality they can interact with a product's primary attributes in three ways:

- *Independence,* having no impact on traditional benefits
- *Dissonance,* diminishing traditional benefits
- *Resonance,* enhancing traditional benefits

Let's consider three "sustainable" laundry detergents that compete with a conventional, middle-of-the-pack product that doesn't promise any environmental or social benefits.

The first is a detergent with natural ingredients that are better for the planet. It's priced slightly higher because the formulation is more expensive to make. But this detergent's natural ingredients don't reduce its traditional benefits—its cleaning ability, stain-removing power, and gentleness. This is a case of independence. The customer gets the same performance the traditional detergent offers (reasons to buy) with the added environmental benefit (reasons to care) but pays a little bit more.

Almost all brand-related social-cause initiatives are a form of independence marketing. J&B Whisky has garnered millions of social media views for an advertisement that promotes diversity

Idea in Brief

The Problem

Many companies overestimate consumers' appetite for sustainable products, flooding the market with offerings that don't sell well.

The Opportunity

By understanding how sustainability features interact with a product's core benefits, companies can devise effective marketing strategies for different consumer segments.

The Solution

Assess whether your sustainable offering's performance is equivalent, inferior, or superior to that of conventional alternatives. Tailor marketing messages to customers according to how they value sustainability versus traditional attributes.

and inclusion through a story about a family accepting a transgender member. Similarly, IBM's support of Girls Who Code, a nonprofit organization dedicated to helping young women enter computer science fields, doesn't directly affect the performance of its consumer and business offerings. In both cases, the brands' social-cause commitments enhance buyers' reasons to care and may influence customer loyalty and sales, but they don't affect product performance.

It's worth noting that when selling offerings with independent sustainability benefits, firms in different industries may be competing for the same dollars. Many customers have a subconscious "sustainability budget" and may be willing to spend only a limited amount of money on sustainable products. So any firm that can provide customers with *greater* sustainability benefits has a potential competitive advantage.

In the second detergent, natural ingredients diminish the product's performance. As a result it suffers from dissonance. Consumers perceive that it is eco-friendly but that it delivers less and costs more than a traditional product. The reasons to care increase, but reasons to buy decrease.

Interestingly, research shows that merely signaling that a product is green can create negative perceptions about it, a phenomenon called "sustainability liability." For instance, environmentally friendly drain openers may be perceived by consumers to be less effective even though they aren't necessarily so, and shoes made with green materials are sometimes wrongly assumed to be less durable. (This perception of liability may change over time, however, as consumers become more accustomed to sustainable products.)

With the third detergent, the product's natural ingredients have unique properties that enhance its cleaning power and gentleness. This is a case of resonance. Consumers' reasons to buy and reasons to care both increase. Makers of resonant products find synergies between sustainability and performance. Revier Cattle Company in Minnesota, for instance, has a program called Total Livestock Care, which focuses on excellent feed (all-natural and with no preservatives, hormones, or additives) and excellent facilities (to reduce stress on cattle). According to blind taste tests done with chefs, restaurateurs, and butchers, these practices have improved the taste of Revier's meat while enabling the company to achieve a sustainability scorecard that's enviable in its industry.

Marketing to Sustainability Segments

The manner in which social and environmental features interact with traditional attributes significantly affects a product's appeal to different consumer groups. However, we find that many companies unwittingly adopt a one-size-fits-all approach to sustainability marketing, which risks alienating certain customers. Brands need to segment their customers by attitudes toward sustainability and tailor their messages accordingly.

A simple and practical way to do that is to divide consumers into three categories. *Greens* (or if your marketing department prefers to use personas, "true believers") place a high value on sustainability, actively seek it in their purchasing, and may sacrifice performance or economy to get it. *Blues* (or perhaps "agnostics") place a moderate value on sustainability and, if they don't need to sacrifice much (or ideally at all) on price and performance, tend to prefer sustainable offerings over alternatives. *Grays* ("disbelievers") don't care about sustainability and may even view it with skepticism. Each kind of consumer requires a different approach.

A customer—whether an individual or a company—may shift consumption profiles from product to product. Someone may be a green consumer in one category (for example, exclusively purchasing clean energy), blue in another (preferring recycled packaging if there's no cost difference), and gray in another, avoiding sustainable cleaning products or construction materials on the assumption that they underperform. Understanding these dynamics is important.

It's also imperative to recognize that making a buying decision is a multifaceted psychological process, one that is not always steered solely by the tangible attributes of products or services. For instance, it may be affected by the phenomenon of *moral licensing*, wherein consumers, having made a significant eco-friendly decision like investing $50,000 in an electric vehicle, become less likely to spend an additional $5 on an ecological product, because they feel they've earned a pass. Similarly, the desire for *social signaling* could drive more-conspicuous sustainable choices like solar roof panels over less visible ones—say, an eco-friendly paper product. It's crucial for marketers and businesses to be aware of such behavioral tendencies. (For more on how biases influence green consumption, see "The Elusive Green Consumer," HBR, July–August 2019.)

In addition, the three types of products all have different playbooks. Let's now look at each one in action.

The Independence Playbook

A B2B client of ours, Georg Fischer (GF), uses renewable materials in all the polyvinyl chloride (PVC) metric pressure pipes, fittings, and valves it produces. The sustainable PVC resin is made using tall oil, a waste product from paper production, reducing manufacturing-related CO_2 emissions by up to 90%, with no impact on product quality and durability.

How should GF communicate about its PVC manufacturing with customers? With gray customers there's no upside in emphasizing sustainability attributes, and so they shouldn't be a focus—particularly since grays may wonder if there's a hidden sustainability price premium or performance cost. However, GF's sustainable manufacturing is a selling point for green and blue customers. With them, GF should underscore that using eco-friendly PVC resin doesn't affect the performance of its pipes, fittings, and valves. For these customers, GF offers science-based, third-party audits of each product's environmental performance over its complete life cycle.

With blue customers it's important to understand their sustainability priorities and gauge your relative contribution to them. Another of our clients, a company that provides energy-efficient milking equipment to the dairy industry, was puzzled by a blue customer that showed little interest in its environmental message. It turned out that the customer was working with its animal-feed and supplements supplier to meet its emissions-reduction goals because cows, not farm equipment, were the main source of its greenhouse gas emissions. Our client's efficient equipment would be of little help in meeting the customer's sustainability goals. The company belatedly realized that, for this customer, it was leading with the wrong message and should have focused instead on the cost savings its equipment promised.

Independence strategies typically offer temporary differentiation advantages. Because customers may choose to get their sustainable benefits from a completely different kind of product, it's difficult to charge a premium for them over the long term. Blue consumers, in particular, will look for the lowest-priced sustainability benefits. If you do charge a premium, be conservative and don't chase excessive margin—and continually reassess your customers' sustainability needs and your competitive situation.

The Dissonance Playbook

Just because dissonant products require customers to accept reduced performance in exchange for sustainability, that doesn't mean their brands will inevitably fail. Firms can profitably sell such products to green consumers and in some instances even to blue ones.

One strategy to broaden the customer base is to attract a subset of blue customers who can be persuaded to accept a performance sacrifice because they stand to gain personally from new benefits tied

Playbooks for Sustainability Success

SUSTAINABLE PRODUCTS CANNOT ALL be marketed in the same way. How their social and environmental benefits interact with traditional product benefits will affect which consumer segments they appeal to and the strategies that work best with them.

	Independence	Dissonance	Resonance
Value proposition	More sustainability with same performance on traditional benefits	More sustainability but lower performance on traditional benefits	More sustainability and greater performance on traditional benefits
Message to customers	"We can help you meet your broader sustainability goals."	"We are in this together, but you need to make a performance sacrifice."	"We've improved performance, and sustainability is an extra benefit."
Customer segments	Green consumers (true believers) and blue consumers (agnostics)	Niche markets— mainly green and some blue consumers	Green and blue consumers as well as gray consumers (disbelievers)
Competitors	Any player providing the same sustainability benefits	Any player providing the same traditional benefits	Any player providing the same traditional benefits
Pricing strategy	Charge temporary price premium if sustainability is a must-have	Charge a premium because green customers are less price-sensitive	Go high; performance is enhanced

to a firm's sustainability actions. Take Oatly. When its plant-based milk was launched in Europe in 1994 as a lactose-free alternative, its sales stagnated owing to the sticky habits of milk consumers and perceptions of inferior taste. However, in 2014, it shifted its image to a lifestyle brand for the "post-milk generation," using the slogan "It's like milk but made for humans." While tacitly acknowledging that the product might differ in taste and nutrition, Oatly emphasized its sustainable and trendy attributes, making it more appealing to a wider audience. That strategic rebranding paved the way for its successful entry into the U.S. market and in 2022 pushed its global sales to $722 million.

While Oatly made its dissonant product cool to consumers, other companies have had success marketing more-tangible benefits. Toyota's hybrid Prius is an iconic example. Launched in 1997, the Prius was expensive, and some considered it underpowered compared with cars with conventional engines. But the greenest buyers were willing to accept those trade-offs for the environmental benefits it promised, as well as the social signaling that the car's unique silhouette conveyed. In addition, Toyota shrewdly used nonmarket strategies to broaden Prius's appeal in California. It successfully lobbied the state legislature to allow hybrids in high-occupancy-vehicle lanes even with a single occupant. Hybrid owners were also allowed to park for free at some public meters in Los Angeles and other California cities. Those strategies pulled in blue customers. Over time, Toyota improved the Prius and reduced the trade-offs on traditional benefits. In 2022, it sold 2.6 million hybrid vehicles globally across all its brands. To put that number in perspective, Ford sold 4.2 million vehicles of all types in North America that year.

Firms with established brands should be thoughtful in how they position dissonant product extensions. Our advice here is simple: Do an honest assessment of the trade-offs; large trade-offs will be acceptable only to greens, and in that situation marketers should be laser focused on highlighting the new product's sustainability credentials to that segment only. If a firm can leverage new benefits tied to sustainability, as Oatly and Prius did, it can appeal to blue customers as well. Pricing strategy here is straightforward: Because with dissonant products you must focus mostly on green consumers, who have a large appetite for sustainable benefits, you have some leverage to extract a premium. But how big that premium is depends on how much consumers value those benefits.

Firms should also continually scan the market for potential converts—customers who may have previously resisted a dissonant offering but are now willing to accept some sacrifice to achieve their sustainability goals. Maersk, the integrated container logistics firm, is a convert. The firm made a commitment to transport at least 25% of ocean cargo using green fuels, which can cost as much as 54% more than conventional fuels, by 2030. Maersk made that move to achieve its own sustainability goals as well as to support large customers that were frustrated with the lack of options for reducing emissions from transportation.

The Resonance Playbook

Unlike offerings with independence or dissonance, products with resonant sustainability features have much more latitude to target a broad customer base. For the most part, the brand message is all upside: "We give you better performance, and you get sustainability too." Both greens and blues respond well to messages that showcase performance as well as sustainability. While it may seem that you should be able to charge the highest prices for resonant products, keep in mind that they could put off gray customers. With them you must justify premium prices by either highlighting higher traditional benefits or bundling sustainable benefits with traditional benefits.

GEA, a B2B manufacturing client of ours, designs equipment for various industries with a focus on sustainability and cost-efficiency. Its AddCool solution for milk-powder production slashes carbon emissions by 50% to 80% and operating costs by 20% to 30% while preserving product quality. Yet as Nadine Sterley, GEA's chief sustainability officer, notes, adopting these solutions isn't a no-brainer for everyone. Some brands readily integrate them, while others are more cautious.

European customers, mainly greens and some blues, have often paid premium prices for GEA's equipment. However, sustainability is less valued by certain U.S. and Asian clients who tend to be grays. Leading with a sustainability-centric message could turn off those customers, who might think they're shouldering sustainability costs. So GEA fine-tuned its messaging and pricing in those markets, underscoring economic advantages (such as reduced energy and water use) rather than sustainability.

Firms should revisit their overall brand promise if a new sustainability benefit can be tied to an easily recognized traditional one. Reckitt launched a product-line extension of Finish, a leading dishwashing detergent, that was so effective it eliminated the need to rinse dishes before loading. That saves up to 75 liters of water with every wash, a huge sustainability gain, but it also played into Finish's traditional brand promise of delivering exceptional cleaning. Finish thus modified its messaging to give customers "sparkling clean dishes the first time, every time, without the need for pre-rinsing—saving dozens of litres of water per load." Eliminating pre-rinsing is a new traditional benefit that flowed from the pursuit of a sustainability benefit—saving water. It resonates with greens, blues, and even most grays. In its first year touting the new brand promise in Turkey, an initial test market, Finish saw its market share among tier-one brands rise by 27%. Reckitt has since rolled out the product with a similar message in more than half a dozen countries.

One thing to keep in mind is that the three playbooks don't offer the same potential for long-term success. Resonant products undoubtedly hold the greatest promise. They can appeal to all customer segments, positioning firms to use sustainability as a powerful strategic tool. A dissonant approach might work in certain geographies or sectors, but it will remain a niche strategy until greens come to dominate the consumer landscape. Independent products, though offering broader appeal to both greens and blues, could end up vying for consumers' sustainability dollars across different categories.

While we have made marketing the focus of this article, at the core of successful sustainable offerings lies innovation; there's no substitute for it. Thus the real battle for sustainable products won't be waged through advertising or public relations stunts; it will happen in research-and-development labs. There leading firms will craft ground-breaking solutions that not only deliver unparalleled performance but also champion environmental protection and societal well-being.

Originally published in March–April 2024. Reprint R2402E

What Does "Stakeholder Capitalism" Mean to You?

by Lynn S. Paine

THE PAST FEW YEARS have seen an outpouring of articles and statements heralding the arrival of a new and more inclusive form of capitalism, often called "stakeholder capitalism." It promises to bolster companies, improve outcomes for their constituencies, produce better returns for long-term shareholders, and ultimately strengthen the economy and society as a whole. In line with the new ideology, corporate boards and business leaders have been urged to adopt a multistakeholder approach to governance in place of the shareholder-centered one that has guided their work for several decades.

In speaking with hundreds of corporate directors, executives, investors, governance professionals, and academics over the years, I've found wide differences in how stakeholder capitalism is understood. The failure to recognize those differences has been a source of much confusion and disagreement inside companies and in the public debate. The recent controversy over environmental, social, and governance investing is a case in point. In this article I describe four kinds of stakeholder capitalism—*instrumental, classic, beneficial,* and *structural*—which reflect significantly different levels of commitment to the interests of stakeholders and are based on very different rationales. (See the exhibit "Four versions of stakeholder capitalism.")

As more companies embrace stakeholder capitalism, it is important that corporate leaders have a shared understanding of what, exactly, they are embracing. Espousing a commitment to all stakeholders without clarity about what that actually entails puts directors and executives on a collision course with one another when decisions requiring difficult trade-offs among stakeholders' interests arise—as they inevitably do. It also creates expectations among stakeholders that if unfulfilled will fuel cynicism, alienation, and distrust—the opposite of what most proponents of stakeholder capitalism intend. Meanwhile, shareholders are left wondering what this new ideology means for them. This article is intended as a guide to help corporate leaders define what they mean by stakeholder capitalism and thus reduce the risk of such negative consequences.

Instrumental Stakeholderism: Maximizing Long-Term Shareholder Value

This version of stakeholder capitalism holds that considering the interests of all stakeholders can actually help maximize returns to shareholders, because how a company treats its nonshareholder stakeholders can affect shareholder value. Investing in other stakeholders may reduce shareholder value today but pay off for shareholders in the future. Conversely, shortchanging other stakeholders may benefit shareholders for a time but be detrimental to them over a longer period. Thus even corporate leaders whose only objective is maximizing value for shareholders should consider the interests of other stakeholders.

That appears to be the dominant understanding of stakeholder capitalism in much of the investment community today. Certainly recent statements by heads of the "big three" asset managers in the United States—BlackRock, Vanguard, and State Street Global Advisors—seem to reflect this view. In his 2021 letter to CEOs,

Idea in Brief

The Insight

Stakeholder capitalism can take several forms, but few leaders distinguish among them.

The Challenge

The failure of corporate leaders to establish a shared understanding of which form they're embracing leads to confusion and controversy.

The Answer

To reduce the risk of such misalignment, leaders should be clear about which version of stakeholderism they are espousing and what it will take to deliver on that commitment. This article describes the four main types.

BlackRock chairman and CEO Larry Fink stated: "The more your company can show its purpose in delivering value to its customers, its employees, and its communities, the better able you will be to compete and deliver long-term, durable profits for shareholders."

This view recognizes that actions taken today have consequences for tomorrow and that the interests of different stakeholders are often interdependent. Consider the simple example of investing in employees' development. Giving your salespeople time away from their jobs to learn new skills may dampen that quarter's sales, disappointing some shareholders and possibly hurting the stock price. But it will most likely help sales and fuel growth in the future, increasing shareholder value. By the same logic, forgoing such investment may improve the bottom line and benefit shareholders today but lead to declining sales, operational inefficiencies, and ultimately losses in shareholder value that exceed the earlier gains if your sales team's skills become outdated.

An instrumental approach to stakeholders in no way challenges shareholder primacy and is fully consistent with its four main tenets: treating shareholder-value maximization as the corporate objective; prioritizing accountability to shareholders over accountability to other stakeholders; subordinating the preferences of other stakeholders to those of shareholders; and giving shareholders the exclusive right to vote on directors and other governance matters. It differs from traditional shareholder capitalism in just two

Four versions of stakeholder capitalism

Proponents of stakeholderism take varying stances on the strength and basis of their commitment to nonshareholder stakeholders. The spectrum below explains those commitments, from weakest to strongest.

Instrumental	Classic	Beneficial	Structural
Managers should respect stakeholders' interests when doing so will maximize long-term returns to shareholders.	Companies have ethical and legal obligations to stakeholders that must be respected whether or not doing so is likely to maximize shareholder value.	The corporate objective is improving all stakeholders' well-being (rather than just maximizing value for shareholders).	To protect stakeholder interests, stakeholders other than shareholders should have formal powers in corporate governance.

main ways: by giving explicit consideration to other stakeholders' interests, and by assessing shareholder value over a longer period.

Some commentators say those differences are inconsequential. But paying explicit attention to other stakeholders' interests can reveal risks that decision-makers often don't recognize when they're focused narrowly on shareholder value. Indeed, disregard for those interests has led to substantial destruction of shareholder value at numerous companies. Consider the fake-accounts debacle at Wells Fargo and Dieselgate at Volkswagen—to name just two. Had leaders of those companies paid more attention to the interests of constituents who were not shareholders, they might have pursued different practices or strategies and ultimately done a better job for their shareholders.

Paying attention to stakeholder interests and taking a longer view can also reveal strategic opportunities. Corporate leaders narrowly focused on near-term shareholder returns would be unlikely to choose to build a new plant in their distressed home region rather than in a lower-cost location overseas. But Cummins did just that in 2010 when it decided to manufacture its new line of high-speed, low-emissions engines in Seymour, Indiana. Its decision meant that the company would have to make significant investments in the community and its schools—but it also presented an opportunity to raise educational attainment and income levels in the region and create a global hub for advanced manufacturing that would ultimately benefit the company. In 2015 Cummins began producing its new line of engines at the Seymour plant. And thanks in part to its collaboration with other companies and the region's civic and educational leaders, local residents' educational attainment, incomes, and wage rates improved as well.

Challenges for instrumental stakeholderism

This approach promises real benefits for stakeholders and society, but those benefits go only so far. Although it requires corporate leaders to take stakeholders' interests into account, it does not require them to *respect* those interests unless doing so would be financially beneficial for shareholders. From this perspective, an investment in the company's stakeholders, like any other investment, should be pursued only if it increases net present value, and investments in stakeholders that reduce long-term shareholder value should be avoided. While proponents of instrumental stakeholderism tend to focus on win-win examples like the Cummins case, corporate leaders frequently face pressure and opportunities to generate shareholder value in ways that do not benefit all stakeholders and may even do harm to some of them.

The economists Roy Shapira and Luigi Zingales have shown, for example, that polluting the environment, even when it is against the law and harmful to public health, can sometimes maximize long-term value for shareholders. Using information disclosed in numerous lawsuits, they examined the decision DuPont executives made in 1984 regarding perfluorooctanoic acid (PFOA), a toxic chemical used in making Teflon that was seeping into the drinking water of the community where it was manufactured. Documents showed that executives knew about PFOA's toxicity to humans and persistence in the environment. As the authors reported in their paper "Is Pollution Value-Maximizing?," three options were considered: ending production of PFOA, continuing production with measures to abate the harmful emissions, and continuing production without abatement measures. Shapira and Zingales modeled the decision from the perspective of a shareholder-value-maximizing manager using the present value of the long-term costs and benefits to the company associated with each option. Their analysis found that the executives' decision—to continue producing PFOA without abatement—maximized shareholder value, even after taking into account legal liabilities, regulatory sanctions, reputational effects, and other costs to the company over the ensuing 30 years. In other words, the decision was perfectly correct from the perspective of instrumental stakeholderism, because an option that respected other stakeholders' interests would not have maximized long-term shareholder value.

Proponents of instrumental stakeholderism sometimes cite the clarity of its decision rule as one of its principal virtues. But predicting which course of action will most likely maximize long-term shareholder value is fraught with difficulty, especially when it requires putting a monetary value on outcomes such as health, clean air, and justice, which have no market price, or predicting how laws, policies, or public sentiment will evolve over the long term. The longer the time frame, the more speculative the exercise. The rule to maximize long-term shareholder value may be clear on its face, but it does not eliminate difficult trade-offs, and it can sometimes result in serious harm to other stakeholders and society at large.

Classic Stakeholderism: Respecting Stakeholders' Legitimate Claims

This version of stakeholder capitalism holds that at least some stakeholders' interests must be respected as well as considered. It differentiates among interests, prioritizing those protected by ethical or legal norms over those based on wishes or desires. The core idea is that the former, more fundamental, interests give rise to claims whose validity is not contingent on their contribution to shareholder value and underpin obligations to stakeholders that sit alongside financial and strategic imperatives. This type of stakeholderism recognizes that serving stakeholder interests often contributes to shareholder value, but that some stakeholder interests should be addressed even when it doesn't. (I call it "classic" because of its similarity to early expressions of stakeholder theory.)

The idea that corporate leaders are permitted, let alone required, to act in ways that don't necessarily maximize shareholder value may sound like heresy. But that is far from the case. Even the best-known proponent of shareholder primacy, Milton Friedman, acknowledged that shareholder value should be pursued within the rules of society as embodied in law and "ethical custom." In his well-known *New York Times* article of 1970 he defined ethical custom quite narrowly, as requiring only that companies compete "without deception or fraud," but presumably he would have condemned deceiving *any* stakeholders—customers, employees, suppliers, shareholders, or communities—even if it could be shown to create long-term value for shareholders.

A more robust form of this view is found in the Business Roundtable's 1981 statement on corporate responsibility, which declared that "the shareholder must receive a good return but the legitimate concerns of other constituencies also must have the appropriate attention." And the American Law Institute's 1992 *Principles of Corporate Governance: Analysis and Recommendations* explicitly acknowledges that corporate decision-makers may pay heed to ethical considerations in their dealings with the company's stakeholders "even if corporate profit and shareholder gain are not thereby enhanced."

Recent court cases in Delaware go further, suggesting that in certain situations respect for some stakeholder interests may even be a matter of fiduciary duty. The 2021 case against Boeing's board of directors speaks to this point. After two fatal crashes of the 737 MAX narrow-body airliner, shareholders filed suit on behalf of the company, alleging that the board had neglected its duty by failing to oversee and monitor airplane safety. In allowing the case to proceed beyond the pleading phase, the court noted that although certain board and management communications mentioned safety "in name," they were not "safety-centric." That is, they focused on

Defining Terms

HOW THE EXPRESSIONS USED in this article shift meaning depending on the context.

Stakeholder
What this term means and to whom it refers have been topics of much debate. The Darden professor R. Edward Freeman has defined it as "any group or individual who can affect, or is affected by, the achievement of a corporation's purpose." In this article I use it more narrowly to refer to the groups that most companies regard as their core constituencies: customers, employees, suppliers, shareholders, and communities or the general public. A case can certainly be made for other definitions and a more extensive list, including business partners, creditors, governments, the environment, NGOs, and even competitors. For the purposes of this article, however, the narrower understanding will suffice.

Shareholder primacy
This term typically refers to one or more of four propositions: (1) Companies should be run with the sole objective of maximizing returns to shareholders. (2) Boards and managers are, or should be, accountable principally to shareholders. (3) Shareholders have, or should have, the exclusive right to elect

---

the financial, operational, public relations, or legal implications of safety rather than on safety itself.

To be sure, establishing a board's liability for a failure of oversight is extremely difficult, and the case was ultimately settled. For directors and officers, however, the case suggests that due regard for stakeholders' fundamental interests—not just their impact on shareholder value—is increasingly seen as integral to their roles.

Challenges for classic stakeholderism
Compared with instrumental stakeholderism, classic stakeholderism provides much stronger protection for stakeholder and societal interests. As critics of stakeholderism have noted, however, determining which interests must be respected is not always easy.

A useful starting point is the norms of corporate conduct that are widely accepted around the world. They include obeying the law, respecting human rights, being truthful and honest, honoring

directors and vote on other corporate matters. (4) Companies should be run according to shareholders' preferences regarding not just financial returns but also social, political, environmental, and other policy matters. These various meanings are often overlooked in discussions of shareholder primacy, but they are noted in this article when relevant.

Shareholder value

This term most commonly refers to financial returns to shareholders. A widely used metric is total shareholder return (TSR), calculated as the sum of dividends, stock price appreciation, and other payments to shareholders over a given period of time. The term is also used to refer to the economic value of the company—which is not necessarily the same as shareholder value in the first sense. Although any increase in the company's value theoretically benefits shareholders through a rise in the stock price, returns to shareholders can also be increased, at least in the short term, by taking actions that reduce the company's longer-term prospects. A third usage treats shareholder value more broadly, as encompassing other things of importance to shareholders, such as particular business strategies, practices, or policies on environmental, social, or political issues. In this article the term is used in its most common sense, to mean financial returns to shareholders, unless otherwise indicated.

promises, protecting health and safety, and so on. Nevertheless, corporate leaders may face difficult judgments about which interests must be protected. Consider a corporate restructuring that involves mass layoffs. The company could save millions of dollars by eliminating its customary (but legally optional) practice of giving advance notice and severance packages to departing employees. Assume further that eliminating those measures would help management meet the guidance on margins previously announced to shareholders. Some managers would see the approach as perfectly valid, arguing that employees have no legitimate claim to advance notice or severance payments in this situation, while others would find it profoundly unfair to employees and thus inconsistent with the requirements of classic stakeholderism.

An equally if not more vexing challenge for classic stakeholderism is resolving conflicts among competing stakeholder claims. Even if the universe of claims is limited to those based on legal and ethical principles, corporate leaders can face difficult trade-offs. During the early days of the pandemic, for instance, some companies in the food sector were torn between ensuring the safety of employees working in plants plagued by Covid outbreaks and meeting their responsibilities to get food to distributors and consumers. Unlike instrumental stakeholderism, which offers "maximize shareholder value" as an all-purpose decision rule for resolving such dilemmas, classic stakeholderism holds that they can be resolved only through a process of deliberation that weighs and compares competing interests and seeks to minimize harm and maximize human well-being.

Critics of stakeholder theory often point to the lack of a single decision rule for resolving trade-offs as a major shortcoming. Proponents, however, see the demand for such a rule as based on an overly narrow conception of rationality, divorced from the messy realities of corporate leadership. They have a point. By its very nature, the job of corporate leaders entails multiple obligations. It is not possible to say in advance how conflicts should be resolved or whose interests should take priority. Both depend on the facts and circumstances of the situation and the nature of the particular interests at stake.

Beneficial Stakeholderism: Improving Outcomes for Stakeholders

This version of stakeholder capitalism seeks not just to meet stakeholders' basic claims but also to measurably improve their well-being. It comes in part from a belief that optimizing returns for shareholders over the past four decades has led many companies to underinvest in their other constituencies and has caused a disproportionate share of gains to go to the owners of capital. It is also driven by the idea that running companies to improve the lives of all stakeholders will help address some of the large-scale problems and inequities facing society today, thereby helping to protect the long-term health of the economy and quell growing discontent with capitalism.

I call this version "beneficial stakeholderism" because of its similarity to the benefit corporation movement, which includes efforts to certify traditional corporations as so-called B Corps and the adoption of legislation in numerous states and countries permitting businesses to organize themselves as "benefit corporations" or "public benefit corporations." Although the certification standards and statutes vary, they have in common a requirement that the company's directors "balance" or "consider" the interests of its various stakeholders when setting policies and making decisions, and that the company periodically report on its progress in advancing stakeholders' well-being.

Beneficial stakeholderism has certain affinities with the benefit corporation approach to stakeholders, but an organization need not be a benefit corporation or a certified B Corp to adopt its basic tenets. Unilever's actions under the leadership of Paul Polman are an example. During Polman's tenure, from 2009 to 2019, the company pursued an agenda that delivered gains for many of its stakeholders. As detailed in Unilever's 10-year progress report on its Sustainable Living Plan, the company enhanced employees' health and well-being, made its pay system more equitable, paid all employees a living wage, and augmented the livelihoods of more than 800,000 smallholder farmers. It advanced human rights in its supply chain, raised the nutritional value of its products, improved the health and hygiene of more than a billion people, and made progress toward cutting its environmental impact in half by 2030. During roughly the same period, Unilever also delivered a total shareholder return of 290%—well above the median of 165% for 18 consumer goods companies in its peer group.

Beneficial stakeholderism is similar to classic stakeholderism in attributing intrinsic (not just instrumental) value to certain interests of nonshareholder stakeholders. However, it calls for a more expansive commitment to the well-being of stakeholders. For example, classic stakeholderism is concerned with employee safety, equal opportunity, equal pay for equal work, and other interests that are protected by basic legal and ethical norms. Beneficial stakeholderism would add to that list dignity, inclusion, meaningful work, and economic equity in the broad sense—whether employees earn a decent livelihood, receive a fair share of the value they are helping create, and have sufficient opportunities for advancement.

Beneficial stakeholderism is more demanding than classic stakeholderism in other ways as well. It envisions ongoing improvement in the outcomes delivered to stakeholders, thus implying defined goals for each stakeholder group and methods for tracking, measuring, and reporting on those outcomes, along with appropriate compensation and incentive systems. It requires an imaginative approach to strategy in which stakeholder interests are essential building blocks rather than side constraints. And it requires a holistic approach to decision-making and resource allocation. Corporate leaders must view each decision not in isolation but as part of a portfolio of choices aimed at achieving the desired outcomes for all stakeholders.

Like instrumental stakeholderism, beneficial stakeholderism rejects the short-termism of traditional shareholder-value maximization. The two versions diverge, however, in their approach to investment decisions. Instead of allocating resources solely on the basis of likely returns to shareholders, beneficial stakeholderism prioritizes projects with the potential to improve outcomes for multiple stakeholders. Although proponents have not, to my knowledge, spelled out precisely how such decisions should be made, the process presumably involves analyzing the expected impact on each affected stakeholder group and choosing either the project with the greatest benefit in aggregate or the one that by some methodology optimizes results across the groups.

Challenges for beneficial stakeholderism

Although this version of stakeholder capitalism holds out the prospect of ever-improving outcomes for all stakeholders, its critics are right to caution against expecting too much. Like classic stakeholderism, beneficial stakeholderism sometimes entails trade-offs among differing interests. But its concern for a broader set of interests can make those trade-offs even more challenging.

Moreover, there is a real question about how much corporate leaders can invest in their nonshareholder stakeholders without losing shareholder support or running afoul of their fiduciary duties. If, for example, the directors of a traditional Delaware corporation decide to sell the company, they are legally obliged to prioritize shareholders' short-term financial interests. But even when the company is not for sale, legal, economic, competitive, and capital-markets factors often constrain leaders' ability to promote the interests of other stakeholders.

Under Delaware law, considered the gold standard for corporate law in the United States, investments in other stakeholders must have a rational relationship to advancing the interests of the corporation. Commentators often brush off this limitation, noting that courts are reluctant to second-guess a board's business decisions. For conscientious corporate leaders, however, a rational relationship to the corporation's interests is an important benchmark. A proposed investment in nonshareholders that does not advance the interests of the corporation must be justified on some other basis. As noted, it might be required or allowed for legal or ethical reasons, or it could be permitted as a charitable contribution. If it cannot be justified in one of those ways, it is (legally speaking) a waste of corporate assets and grounds for legal action against the company's directors.

A more pressing issue for most corporate leaders is not what the law allows but what is realistic given the company's economic and competitive situation. Even stakeholder interests that are directly related to the business can be addressed only up to a point. Customers, for instance, almost always want better quality, better service, and lower prices, but a company's ability to satisfy those desires is not infinite. Investing more in customers typically means investing less in something else. And whether it is a traditional corporation or a benefit corporation, a company can undermine its own viability if its generosity to customers (or any other stakeholders) results in too many loss-making transactions. Many factors—the company's strategy, the expectations of other stakeholders, what resources are available, what competitors are doing, how the industry is changing—affect how much corporate leaders can invest in any one stakeholder group. Even for fast-growing companies in thriving industries, delivering on a multistakeholder strategy can be difficult. For distressed companies and those in low-growth or declining industries, it is even more so.

Corporate leaders' ability to invest in other stakeholders ultimately depends on shareholders' willingness to support those investments. Shareholders who disagree with how resources are being allocated may sell their shares. If enough of them do so, the company's stock price will fall. If the drop is severe or prolonged, the company may become the target of a proxy fight or a takeover bid. Whatever decision- making discretion the legal system gives corporate leaders, their actual choices are constrained by the preferences of shareholders who, as noted, have ultimate power over the company's direction through their rights to buy and sell shares, elect directors, vote on major transactions, and challenge directors in court.

In summary, beneficial stakeholderism holds promise, but corporate leaders who embrace it face a challenging path. In comparison with instrumental and classic stakeholderism, beneficial stakeholderism envisions a more significant shift away from traditional shareholder-value maximization in how companies deploy resources and distribute the value they create, with a greater share of both going to nonshareholder stakeholders. But, as discussed, limits on their ability to advance other stakeholders' interests are real. Only 13% of directors responding to a recent survey by PwC agreed strongly that climate goals should be a priority even if they affect short-term financial performance. Perhaps that's because few investors in public companies appear willing to forgo meaningful returns for a greener planet or a more equitable society.

Structural Stakeholderism: Increasing Stakeholder Power

The three versions of stakeholderism discussed so far all focus on the first pillar of shareholder primacy: Maximizing value for shareholders is (or should be) a corporation's principal objective. They all call for refinements or changes to that objective or how it is implemented, and they are similar in leaving the traditional governance structures and processes that define the balance of power between shareholders and other stakeholders largely intact. That is to say, they all accept another pillar of shareholder primacy: Shareholders are (or should be) the only constituency with a formal voice in corporate governance. A fourth version—which I term "structural stakeholderism"—calls for giving nonshareholder stakeholders voting or other powers in the governance process. Advocates of this version seek to hard wire the interests of other stakeholders into the process, rather than relying on corporate directors and business leaders to take them into account, typically by giving those stakeholders a defined role in selecting directors or formal representation on corporate boards.

Where this idea has been widely implemented, notably in Europe, employees are the stakeholder group (other than shareholders) that is most often given board representation. Germany's two-tiered board system is an example. By law and tradition one-third to one-half of the directors on the supervisory boards of German companies are elected by employees and the rest by shareholders. Other European countries take other approaches to employee participation. Although rare in the United States, employee representation on boards is not unheard of. A 1919 Massachusetts law (still in effect) permitted manufacturing companies to adopt bylaws empowering employees to elect one or more directors, and some unions have secured a seat on company boards. The board of Delta Air Lines, for example, includes a pilot nominated by the governing body of its pilot association. In the past few years more than a dozen shareholder proposals about adding nonmanagement employees to boards have been voted on (and gotten scant support) at large U.S. companies, and several bills in the U.S. Senate would give employees of large companies the right to elect a certain percentage of the board.

The appointment of directors who represent the public interest has also been proposed from time to time. The idea gained currency among law and business academics in the United States in the 1970s, following a spate of corporate failures and scandals. It was actually tried on the boards of Irish banks that received government bailouts during the global financial crisis of 2008. Other commentators have proposed that customers, communities, and taxpayers or other stakeholders have board representation. For some, the term "stakeholder capitalism" itself implies that corporate boards should comprise representatives of various stakeholder groups.

Most advocates for adding stakeholder representatives to boards or extending voting rights beyond shareholders claim that more-robust involvement of other constituencies would strengthen companies' ability to create long-term value by boosting productivity, enhancing employee engagement, or sparking innovation. But for most, those are secondary consequences. The principal goal is to protect the interests of nonshareholder stakeholders and increase the weight given to them in corporate decision-making.

Challenges for structural stakeholderism

The call to add representatives of employees or other stakeholders to corporate boards raises fundamental questions about the nature of boards and the duties of directors—and about the basis of directors' authority to govern. Although directors are sometimes referred to as shareholders' "representatives"—and, as noted, are elected by shareholders—they are legally more akin to trustees for the institution than to delegates representing a particular constituency. That is why other shareholders may protest when an activist hedge fund negotiates a seat on the board for its own nominee or offers additional compensation to that director for achieving its goals. As fiduciaries, directors owe care and loyalty to the corporation as a whole and are obliged to exercise independent judgment on its behalf—not to do the bidding of a subset of shareholders.

Under the traditional legal model, a corporate board is thus closer to a fiduciary board than to a constituency board. Those two orientations lead to very different mindsets and very different requirements for director effectiveness. Fiduciaries for the institution must understand the interests of multiple constituencies and how they relate to the business as a whole. To maintain their objectivity, they need to keep some distance from interested parties seeking to exert influence. By comparison, representatives of a constituency are expected to engage closely with its members, carry out their wishes, and advocate for their interests. Fiduciary directors and constituency directors can thus take very different stances on issues that come before the board.

Few if any proposals to add employees or other stakeholders to corporate boards raise this issue explicitly, but many of them seem to envision those boards as constituency boards comprising representatives of various stakeholder groups. Although constituency boards are appropriate for some organizations, the model has troubling implications for business corporations. Perhaps the most worrisome is the potential effect on the speed and coherence of decision-making. If the principal duty of directors is to serve the interests of the groups they represent rather than the interests of the company, the prospect of lengthy negotiations and contentious standoffs quickly arises. Decisions about strategy, investments, leadership, acquisitions, divestments, restructuring, and the like must often be made quickly. In a rapidly changing business environment, taking time to solicit the views of various stakeholder groups and to negotiate a resolution of the differences among them may not be feasible. Moreover, without a shared duty to the company to anchor and focus the negotiations, the odds of a suboptimal result are high.

The concept of stakeholder boards runs counter to the ideals of director independence that are at the core of good governance today. For advocates of stakeholder boards, having an interest in the business as an employee, a customer, a supplier, or another constituent is a qualification for service. But it can also compromise a director's judgment and undermine boards' ability to make overall value-creating decisions. Proponents of stakeholder boards envision them as collaborative bodies working toward a single purpose, whereas skeptics envision them as thickets of competing claims that breed distrust and impair decision-making. Before embracing stakeholder boards, it would be wise to clarify the duties of their members and consider how they are likely to function in practice.

Stakeholder capitalism can be more or less than meets the eye—and more or less of a challenge to shareholder primacy—depending on which version is being considered. Each one involves a distinctive set of commitments and challenges, and each has very different practical implications for how companies and their boards function.

Corporate leaders need a clear understanding of what those implications are. They also need to be honest about what their version can actually deliver for stakeholders, what it can deliver for society, and what it means for shareholders. We have passed the point at which concern about conflicts can be brushed off with easy appeals to a presumed long-term harmony of interests among shareholders, stakeholders, and society. The time has come to clarify what we mean by "stakeholder capitalism."

Originally published in September–October 2023. Reprint R2305H

Use Strategic Thinking to Create the Life You Want

by Rainer Strack, Susanne Dyrchs, and Allison Bailey

IN TIMES OF CRISIS, many of us ponder existential questions about health, security, purpose, career, family, and legacy. However, more often than not, such contemplation is short-lived. The demands of everyday life—the here and now—can overwhelm us, leaving little time to think about the long term and what we are working toward. As a result, when faced with life decisions both big and small, we are left with nothing to guide us but emotion or intuition.

The corporate equivalent, of course, is attempting to run a business without a strategy, which every HBR reader knows is a losing proposition. But as longtime consultants to organizations around the world, we wondered: Could we adapt the model for strategic thinking that we use with institutional clients to help individuals design better futures for themselves? The answer is yes, and the result is a program that we call Strategize Your Life. We've tested it with more than 500 people—including students, young professionals, middle-aged employees and managers, C-suite executives, board members, and retirees—to help them develop their individual life strategies.

You can create a life strategy at any time, but it can feel especially appropriate at certain milestones—a school graduation, the start of your first job, a promotion, becoming an empty-nester, retiring—or after a major life event, such as a health scare, a divorce, the loss of a job, a midlife crisis, or the death of a loved one. When you have a strategy, you will be better able to navigate all those transitions and difficult moments, building resilience and finding more joy and fulfilment while minimizing stress. This article will help you get started.

A Surprising Symmetry

Every corporate strategy project is different. But the hundreds that we've conducted for large organizations have had commonalities, including the use of certain methodologies and tools. We typically work through seven steps, each guided by a question:

1. How does the organization define success?

2. What is our purpose?

3. What is our vision?

4. How do we assess our business portfolio?

5. What can we learn from benchmarks?

6. What portfolio choices can we make?

7. How can we ensure a successful, sustained change?

These steps can be easily adapted to an individual:

1. How do I define a great life?

2. What is my life purpose?

3. What is my life vision?

4. How do I assess my life portfolio?

5. What can I learn from benchmarks?

6. What portfolio choices can I make?

7. How can I ensure a successful, sustained life change?

Idea in Brief

The Problem

The demands of everyday life—the here and now—can overwhelm us, leaving little time to think about the long term and what we are working toward. As a result, when faced with life decisions both big and small, we are left with nothing to guide us but emotion or intuition.

The Solution

In corporate strategy projects, executive leadership teams work through a series of questions to determine how their businesses can succeed. Individuals can use a similar process to figure out how to live a meaningful life. It starts with defining what makes a great life for you and then outlining your purpose and vision.

The Payoff

The Strategize Your Life program has been tested with more than 500 people around the world. With a few hours of work, you can develop a personal life strategy and summarize it on a single page.

As the former head of strategy for a U.S.-based *Fortune* 50 company told us, "Knowing the right questions is much harder than having the answers." Just as corporate strategy is an integrated set of choices that positions a company to win, *life strategy* is an integrated set of choices *that positions a person to live a great life.* What's more, we can apply tools from classic organizational strategy and other realms to help you find answers to the seven questions above and make better decisions.

Critics might say that you can't transfer concepts from business to life. In the 1960s there were similar concerns about whether strategy ideas from the military and politics could apply to the corporate world. The management guru Peter Drucker even changed the title of his 1964 book from *Business Strategy* to *Managing for Results* because everyone he and his publisher asked told them that strategy belonged to those realms, not to business. Yet we've also seen business-world principles employed to improve people's self-management. For example, in their bestselling book *Designing Your Life*, Stanford University's Bill Burnett and Dave Evans modified the design thinking they used in software development to help individuals.

From corporate strategy to life strategy

The questions that organizations use to set a course for the future can be easily adapted to help individuals do the same.

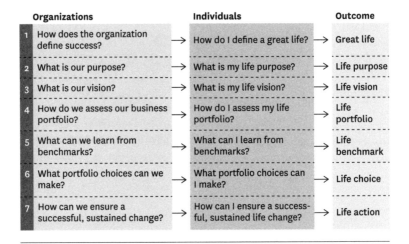

	Organizations		Individuals		Outcome
1	How does the organization define success?	→	How do I define a great life?	→	Great life
2	What is our purpose?	→	What is my life purpose?	→	Life purpose
3	What is our vision?	→	What is my life vision?	→	Life vision
4	How do we assess our business portfolio?	→	How do I assess my life portfolio?	→	Life portfolio
5	What can we learn from benchmarks?	→	What can I learn from benchmarks?	→	Life benchmark
6	What portfolio choices can we make?	→	What portfolio choices can I make?	→	Life choice
7	How can we ensure a successful, sustained change?	→	How can I ensure a successful, sustained life change?	→	Life action

Strategize Your Life is our attempt to do the same for strategic thinking in a concrete, step-by-step way. We believe it can lead you to new insights on how you define and find your great life. Our goal is to give your emotion and intuition an analytical partner.

In surveying our workshop and coaching session participants, we found that, in the past, only 21% had outlined what a great life means to them, 9% had identified their purpose, 12% had set a vision for their life, 17% had created concrete goals and milestones, and a paltry 3% had developed what could be called a life strategy. These are critically important issues that very few of us are spending enough time on.

As Martha, a 26-year-old graduate student, explained, "Life keeps taking shape. . . . When all the Christmas parties and weddings and trips are suddenly over, you ask yourself, Have I really lived or has life just happened to me?" She was eager to be more proactive. "What better help is there than a high-level plan for life?" she asked.

"Not to strictly follow it and forbid life to unfold, but to have a common thread. What should my story be? What should I have experienced so that in the end I can say to myself, 'I have lived'?"

Unlike most self-help books, we don't present one golden path to happiness or life satisfaction. Because everyone is unique, we give you the tools to find your own path in a seven-step life strategy process. In step 1 you define what a great life means for you. In step 2 you outline your purpose; in step 3 your life vision. Step 4 is a portfolio analysis of how you spend your 168-hour week, while step 5 involves setting life satisfaction benchmarks. In step 6 you incorporate the results of the first five steps and determine your choices and potential changes in your life, and in step 7 you map out a plan for putting your choices into action. We recommend that you take notes throughout so that, by the end, you can put an initial version of your life strategy on a single page. (To help, we created a life strategy worksheet, which you can access using the QR code near the end of this article and you should fill out after you've gone through all the steps.)

This work may seem daunting, but in practice it should take you only a few hours. That said, it might not be easy. You will have to challenge yourself and go beyond the obvious. But you shouldn't give up, because the answers you'll discover are so worthwhile. After all, what's more important than your life? Commit to thinking strategically about it, look forward to the insights you will gain, and enjoy the journey.

The Seven Steps

The process begins with a simple yet profound question:

1. How do I define a great life?

The starting point of any corporate strategy process is to define fundamental metrics for success. For instance, does the organization want its strategy to focus on driving sales, shareholder value, or positive societal impact?

What are the right metrics in an individual's life? Our social norms and hierarchies might suggest we measure ourselves with money, fame, and power. But studies have shown that money leads to greater happiness only to the extent that our basic needs are met, after which its returns diminish or even plateau. Other research shows many of us are on a "hedonic treadmill": After we get a pay raise, are promoted, or purchase something that triggers a pleasurable high, we return to our original level of happiness. And then there is social comparison—no matter what you achieve, someone will always be richer, more famous, or more powerful than you.

The ancient Greeks saw two main dimensions of a great life: *hedonia* (a focus on pleasure) and *eudaimonia* (a focus on virtues and on meaning). More recently, scholars have pointed to the importance of social connection. A study of more than 27,000 people in Asia found a strong correlation between being married and being satisfied with life, while a study that has followed 268 Harvard College men from 1938 to the present, and was expanded to include their children and wives, as well as a study that has followed 456 residents of inner-city Boston since the 1970s, also expanded to include children and wives, found that meaningful relationships were the key driver of long-term happiness. The late Harvard Business School professor Clayton Christensen agreed: In his classic HBR article "How Will You Measure Your Life?" he wrote, "I've concluded that the metric by which God will assess my life isn't dollars but the individual people whose lives I've touched."

A framework that includes all these factors—hedonic, eudemonic, and relational—is the PERMA model, introduced by Martin Seligman, the founder of positive psychology and a University of Pennsylvania professor, in his 2011 book, *Flourish*. Other researchers later developed it into PERMA-V, which stands for Positive emotions (frequent feelings of pleasure and contentment), Engagement (being in the flow, losing track of time), Relationships (mutual feelings of caring, support, and love), Meaning (contributing to making the world a better place), Achievement (striving for success or mastery, reaching goals), and Vitality (being healthy and energetic).

To determine what makes a great life for you, start with each element in PERMA-V, or even add your own categories, such as autonomy or spirituality. Then rate each one's importance to you on a scale from 0 (not important) to 10 (very important). Try to recall periods of deep satisfaction in your past and consider what triggered them. In the first step of strategy projects, we conduct a comprehensive analysis of the status quo. So, you should also rate your current satisfaction with each dimension on a scale from 0 (not at all satisfied) to 10 (very satisfied). This quick assessment will give you a rough idea of how you define a great life and initial ideas about what you need to change.

2. What is my life purpose?
For a corporate strategy to be successful, it must be anchored to the organization's purpose, which lies at the intersection of What are we good at? and What does the world need?, and takes into account, What are our values? and What excites us? Using these questions, we've helped companies around the world develop purpose statements. A purpose statement serves as an important guardrail for your strategy and is a North Star for your organization.

The same questions can be used to find your life purpose. Ask yourself, What am I good at? Think about situations at work or in other areas of life in which you have demonstrated critical strengths such as creativity, teamwork, or communication. Then ask, What are my core values? Think about critical decisions you've made and principles you hold dear that have provided direction, such as honesty, fairness, or integrity.

There are dozens of online lists and tests to help you consider your most important values. The next question is, Which activities light me up? Perhaps your answers include mentoring, problem-solving, or engaging with different types of people. Finally, ask, What need can I help address in the world? It could be one of the 17 Sustainable Development Goals of the United Nations, such as health, education, gender equality, or climate action, or it could be something much more general, such as love, kindness, trust, or security.

In the purpose-defining stage of strategy projects, we conduct belief audits to get input from many stakeholders. Do the same. Ask friends or family members what your strengths are, what values you live by, what things excite you, and what need you might help fill.

Draw from your own answers and theirs to draft a purpose statement, and then ask for feedback on it. Or you can engage ChatGPT in an interactive dance, using the answers to the four questions as input to help you develop your purpose statement, as Tom, a climate physicist, did in one of our recent workshops.

When Joudi, a Kurdish refugee from Syria currently living in Germany, went through this exercise, he identified his core strengths as ambition, passion, and hunger for knowledge. His core values were justice, peace, family, and charity. He said he was most excited by innovation, neurosurgery, and entrepreneurship (notably his experiences selling accessories as a street vendor in Istanbul and founding a multilingual AI-powered integration support platform for Ukrainians who had fled their country for Germany). As for the world needs he wanted to address, Joudi cited health care, freedom, and equality. In the end, he wrote this purpose statement: "Remain medically passionate, willing to learn, entrepreneurial, and strong-willed to drive medical innovation and create equitable access to health care for people."

A chief human resources officer at a global industrial company wanted to step down from her current role but was unsure whether she should look for a similar role in another company or do something completely different. She went through the seven steps and came up with a simple purpose statement, "To help and lead others to aspire," through which she realized that she did want another senior HR role, just in a different company.

There are other methods for defining one's life purpose, of course. But it's important to find the time and a way to do it. We've seen some workshop participants sharpen their existing purpose ideas, while others have had a real "aha" moment, finally understanding what they were meant to do. Purpose guides your life strategy.

3. What is my life vision?
The next step in building a corporate strategy is to set out a vision for the future. We typically ask leadership teams where they want their organization to be—in terms of innovation, growth, product portfolio, market presence, etc.—in five to 10 years. Often we have them

ask themselves questions like, What newspaper headline about our company would we like to read a decade from now?

Individuals should also strive to envision who they want to become in the years ahead. As the Stoic philosopher Seneca said, "If you do not know which port you are sailing to, no wind is favorable." At the same time, you want to remain open to surprises and serendipity. Seneca commented on this as well: "Luck is what happens when preparation meets opportunity." Strategizing your life is the preparation.

So, ask yourself: What story would I like people to tell about me five to 10 years from now? What would I do if money wasn't an issue? What will the 80-year-old me not want to have missed in life? Your purpose and your strengths might also trigger some ideas about your vision.

For this step we have used a photo-sorting exercise similar to what our corporate clients use in branding and innovation strategy projects. Out of 180 photos, workshop participants select two to four that best represent their personal and professional vision—what one person described as a "mood board."

In both business and individual life strategy, a vision can give you focus. Jim, who will soon be a doctor, had a purpose statement that was rather general: "Bring people together and share passions." His vision was more concrete and specific: "To create spaces for more social encounters, such as a medical practice with a shared coffee shop, and to get involved in homeless medicine." Your vision should be equally descriptive.

You might end up with a short list of bullet points or a one-sentence summary of your vision. No matter how you capture it, a vision statement can be powerful in guiding your life. An example we love comes from our colleague Sebastian when he was 14. After a poor math test result, his teacher told him, "Teaching you is a waste of time" and warned he'd never get a high school diploma. For the next couple of years Sebastian took that to heart, skipped school, and started working as a bricklayer. Eventually, however, he decided to make a change, and it began with this vision statement: "I will go to university and get a PhD and then go back to my math teacher—all in the next 10 years." He did just that, graduating summa cum laude with a PhD in economics, and in another 10 years he was a managing director and a partner at BCG.

4. How do I assess my life portfolio?

Companies typically use portfolio analysis to assess their business units on key parameters such as market growth or share and to decide where to invest capital. BCG is well-known for its 2×2 growth-share matrix.

But what is the equivalent of a business unit in life? We focus on six strategic life areas (SLAs): relationships; body, mind, and spirituality; community and society; job, learning, and finances; interests and entertainment; and personal care. We then subdivide the six SLAs into 16 strategic life units (SLUs). (For a full list of the SLUs, see the exhibit "The key areas of life.")

And what are the equivalents of capital expenditures in life? Time, energy, and money. A week has 168 hours. How do you spend them? With your significant other, with family, at work, playing sports, at church, getting a good night's rest?

Look back at the past year, including holidays, and assess how much time you spent on each of the 16 SLUs in an average week. When an activity crosses categories, split the time between them. For example, if you went jogging with your significant other for one hour a week, allocate half an hour to the significant other SLU and half an hour to the physical health/sports SLU. Next, rate all 16 SLUs on a scale of 0 to 10 based on how important they are to you. Then rate the satisfaction you derive from each on the same scale. (This goes one level deeper than the similar PERMA-V exercise.)

Now sketch out your own 2×2; we call it the Strategic Life Portfolio. But instead of mapping growth against share, you will put the importance of each SLU on the y-axis and the satisfaction it brings on the x-axis. Plot each SLU with a bubble, making the size of the bubble roughly proportional to the percentage of time in a week you spend on it.

In the top-left quadrant, you will find the SLUs of high importance and low satisfaction. These are areas of high urgency, because

The key areas of life

People spend their time, energy, and money in six strategic life areas, which can be subdivided into 16 strategic life units. Think about how much time you currently spend on each and rank both its importance and the satisfaction it gives you using a 0–10 scale.

Strategic life areas	Strategic life units	Descriptions
1. Relationships	Significant other	Time with partner, dates
	Family	Engaging with kids, parents, siblings
	Friendship	Time with friends
2. Body, mind, and spirituality	Physical health/sports	Exercise, physical therapy
	Mental health/mindfulness	Psychotherapy, meditation
	Spirituality/faith	Religious practice
3. Community and society	Community/citizenship	Membership in local clubs, jury duty
	Societal engagement	Volunteering, activism
4. Job, learning, and finances	Job/career	Work
	Education/learning	Classes, training
	Finances	Planning, investing
5. Interests and entertainment	Hobbies/interests	Reading, collectibles
	Online entertainment	Social media, TV, gaming
	Offline entertainment	Vacations, theater, sporting events
6. Personal care	Physiological needs	Eating, sleeping
	Activities of daily living	Commuting, housework

you care about these activities deeply but aren't focusing on them enough to get the most out of them. The SLUs in the top-right quadrant also deserve some attention: You want to keep devoting significant time and energy to your most important and highest-satisfaction activities, and invest less in those that are less important (bottom left and right).

Finally, look at your entire 2×2 and ask yourself: Does my current portfolio of SLUs put me on the right track to support my purpose and achieve my vision? Does it bring me closer to how I define a great life? Where can I save and reallocate my time? Just

A sample strategic life portfolio

This 2x2 shows that the subject needs to spend more time and energy on his significant other, mental health/mindfulness, societal engagement, and education/learning SLUs. He should spend less time on online entertainment— an area of low importance.

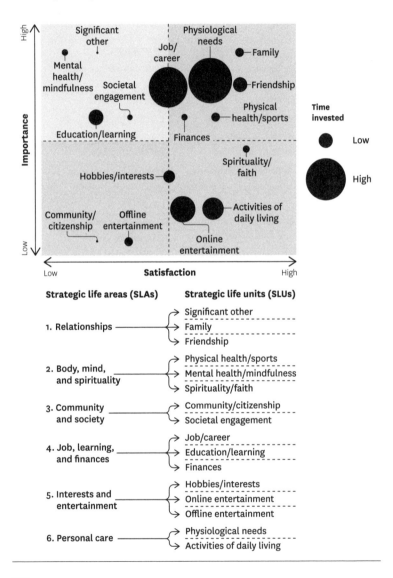

as in corporate strategy projects, you want to set some high-level priorities—rather than a detailed plan—for investments of your time, energy, and money.

When Toni, an engineer, completed this exercise, he saw four areas for urgent improvement in the top-left quadrant: significant other (since he didn't have one), mental health/mindfulness, societal engagement, and education/learning. His job/career SLU was split between two quadrants, and he was spending too much time on online entertainment, which charted in the bottom-right quadrant. It became clear to Toni what he needed to change.

5. What can I learn from benchmarks?

In almost every strategy project, we do a best practice and benchmarking analysis to understand what we can learn from leading companies. We can do the same for individuals by looking at role models and then, more importantly, at the research on life satisfaction.

Ask yourself: Who conducts their personal and professional life in a way I admire? Maybe it is a coworker caring for his bedridden parent, the mother of three at your kids' school who also manages payroll for a *Fortune* 500 company, or your religious leader who lives his purpose. Ask yourself what makes them admirable, and what choices they would make if they were in your shoes.

Now consider what scientific studies tell us about life satisfaction—not anecdotally but across large populations. We already mentioned the Harvard and Asia studies. One of the largest studies worldwide on life satisfaction is the German Socio-Economic Panel survey, which covered almost 100,000 people from 1984 to 2019, gathering more than 700,000 completed responses. It found that significant others, children, friends, sports, spirituality, community involvement, salaries, savings, and nutrition all contribute to life satisfaction. Not surprisingly, health problems have a very negative impact, and you can find an optimum amount of time to spend on leisure and sleep.

Other studies have found that proven life enhancers include practicing kindness, mindfulness, meditation, and gratefulness; cultivating more humor and laughter; dedicating time to learning; and

Benchmarking life satisfaction

One way to explore best practices is to understand where other people spend their time, energy, and money—and whether they report being satisfied with their lives. Longitudinal data from the German Socio-Economic Panel (SOEP) survey of almost 100,000 people from 1984 to 2019 is one source to reference. This chart shows one person's life satisfaction over time, with their satisfaction score reflecting changes to their baseline. Note that correlation does not equal causation.

Life satisfaction score as compared to baseline score **(B)**, by strategic life area(s)

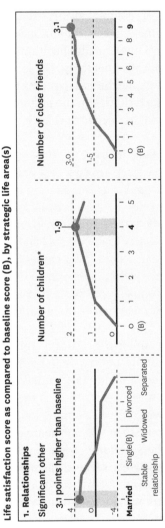

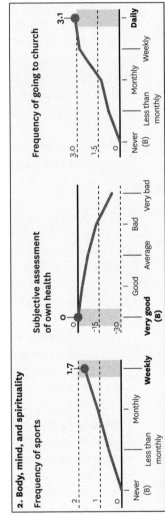

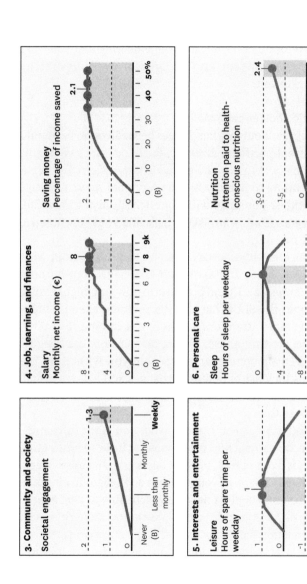

3. Community and society
Societal engagement

4. Job, learning, and finances
Salary
Monthly net income (€)

Saving money
Percentage of income saved

5. Interests and entertainment
Leisure
Hours of spare time per weekday

6. Personal care
Sleep
Hours of sleep per weekday

Nutrition
Attention paid to health-conscious nutrition

* If household income per person won't change.
Life satisfaction on a scale fromn 0–100.

developing a growth mindset (that is, believing your abilities and life can improve through effort and persistence).

As you do this work, it's important to understand and learn from what has worked for others, while also remembering that you can't just copy and paste someone else's approach. Your life strategy should be unique to you.

6. What portfolio choices can I make?

Corporate strategy is about making choices between options: Should we keep our current portfolio, diversify, focus, acquire a company, or enter a new market? In life, the equivalent questions are: What happens if I continue to live my life the way I am now? What if I change my priorities? Equipped with your definition of a great life, your purpose, your vision, your SLU ratings, and your benchmarks, you are ready to find out.

Go back to the great-life exercise in step 1 and think about what you can do for your areas of dissatisfaction. Review your purpose and vision from steps 2 and 3 and brainstorm how you might realize them. Think about the SLUs that step 4's portfolio exercise identified as needing more attention, and how you can improve satisfaction or reallocate time there. Then consider how the insights gleaned from step 5's benchmarks can help you with all of the above. From this long list of potential changes and actions—small and large—select several that will best move you toward a great life, and commit to them.

Now you need to be specific about what you want to change. Examples from our workshop attendees include reconnecting with three friends from school, visiting one's grandpa every week, engaging in a weekly micro-adventure with one's significant other, changing jobs, committing to a new sleep schedule, trying a meditation app, starting a gratitude journal, spending more time with one's kids, exercising every day, supporting refugees, starting a social business, practicing religion again, dedicating 15 minutes to learning every day, switching college majors, converting a van into a camper to travel, and moving abroad. The possibilities are endless.

On the other hand, you have only 168 hours each week, which means you must reduce, outsource, or bundle existing activities, or make them more efficient through productivity strategies and tools. For example, when you work out with your boyfriend or volunteer for a good cause with your friends, you are bundling sports and significant other or societal engagement and friendship. Life strategy is about setting priorities; it is not about filling every waking minute. Remember to reserve space in your calendar for downtime as well. Researchers at the University of Pennsylvania's Wharton School and UCLA's Anderson School of Management found that people are happiest when they have two to five hours of free time each day.

When Judi, a workshop attendee, finished making her list of actions, she commented, "If I change all this, I will be a different person in a few weeks." Your life strategy could involve big steps like starting a business, traveling the world (as one of us did), or setting up an NGO, or it could involve a small step like meeting for coffee every week with people you care about. Even a small change can have a big impact in two key ways. First, if you do it over and over again, you take advantage of the compound growth rate. Second, you are a node in a network of people, so your change not only affects those close to you but also ripples outward. After all, sometimes big changes are triggered by small, seemingly insignificant actions—the famous butterfly effect. For example, research has shown that doing just 15 minutes of physical activity a day increases life expectancy by three years (despite amounting to only about half a year of time investment). Exercise also gives you a dopamine boost, improving your mood, which benefits those around you and makes you more productive at work, potentially leading to new outputs that greatly impact the lives of others.

If you know which strategic life unit needs work but don't know what changes to make, dig deeper and develop a substrategy for that unit—a job/career strategy, a family strategy, a mental health/mindfulness strategy, and so on—just as each business unit does with the overarching corporate strategy.

For example, to develop a job/career strategy, ask yourself the following questions: How does my current job support my purpose and vision? Does my current job give me a sense of achievement and engagement (two of the six great-life dimensions)? How does my current job align with the strengths I identified in the purpose step? Finally, look for benchmarking data, such as BCG's Decoding Global Ways of Working study, where we list the top 10 criteria of great jobs according to more than 200,000 respondents. Again, rate how your job measures up to these criteria. The answers to these questions will give you an idea of how to move forward in your career.

7. How can I ensure a successful, sustained life change?

Change is not easy. Need proof? More than 40% of Americans set New Year's resolutions each January, and reports indicate that more than 90% fail to follow through on them.

Many companies, such as Google, ensure successful implementation of the strategies they've outlined by using OKRs (objectives and key results). OKRs are focused, ambitious, output-oriented, flexible, measurable, and transparent.

We recommend doing the same for each of the changes you committed to in step 6. Define the broad objective and the date by which you want to achieve it. Then break down each of those objectives into a few key results or action items, again with deadlines. Consider adding them directly to your calendar. If you are unsure about implementing a big move in your life, experiment. For example, Toni identified mental health/mindfulness as a high priority, so he might set an objective of "Download an app and try meditation techniques for 10–15 minutes a day (finish by the end of November)." He could then break it down into two key results: (1) review meditation apps and get started (first week of November), and (2) try an app for three weeks, review the experience, and make it a daily habit (last three weeks of November).

There are many ways that companies hold themselves to OKRs. Here, we focus on three of them. *Anchoring* means sharing your plan, as Google does by making its OKRs public. Who will you tell about your plan or ask to join you on your journey? Strategy projects always involve small teams, so consider not only seeking input from others but also inviting one or two people to work on their own life strategies and then workshop everyone's results as a group. *Consequences* means setting up incentives for achievement, such as bonuses for success or penalties for failure. How will you reward yourself when you've successfully changed an aspect of your life, and what will the consequences be if you don't? And *check-ins* means routinely stepping back, refining and adjusting your efforts, and celebrating your achievements, as agile project development teams do. When each week can you spend 15 minutes to review and update your life strategy?

Toni, for example, might tell a friend to hold him to his changes, promise to donate a significant amount of money to a charitable cause if he doesn't stick to them, and schedule a weekly check-in with himself every Sunday before his study session.

Your One-Page Life Strategy

Often, the seeming enormity of an important task—like life strategy development—is what stops us from doing it. So, to make what seems impossible possible, we recommend putting your entire life strategy on a single sheet of paper. We borrowed this idea from one-page summaries we have used in past strategy projects, and we saw it with Craig Perrett, a leadership coach who helps very senior executives at BCG manage their time after a successful career. If you have finished the exercises in this article, you can easily fill out the worksheet. Scan this QR code to download the pdf.

To start, write down what defines a great life for you. Next, record your strengths, your values, what lights you up, and what the world needs, and then add your purpose statement that incorporates those ideas. Third, summarize your life vision. Fourth, refer to that 2×2 you sketched and note the SLUs that are high priorities for action or that you spend too much time on. Next, write down the changes you'd like to make and commit to. Finally, for each of those changes, list an objective and two to three key results with deadlines, and then note the anchors, the consequences, and the check-in plan to make the change stick.

This page is your first minimum viable life strategy. As with corporate strategy, it needs to be reviewed, adjusted, and updated on a regular basis. Proprietary data from BCG suggests that 50% of companies review their strategy once a year, and 20% more than once a year—what we call *always-on strategy development*. Likewise, in addition to your weekly 15-minute check-in, we recommend scheduling a longer, one- to two-hour review session with yourself, or with the life strategy group you started with other people, every six to 12 months. Review all seven steps, consider setbacks or shifting circumstances, and adjust accordingly.

The chief human resources officer we mentioned earlier puts her one-pager on top of all the papers on her desk. She looks at it every day to reinforce her belief in what makes a great life and to ensure she executes on her strategy for achieving it; when she has an idea for refinement, she writes it down. You can try that, too. A couple we worked with, who wanted to develop life strategies in tandem, went so far as to document their life purposes and goals with photos and notes in a picture frame. They hung it on the wall of their home, a daily reminder of where they want to go both together and as individuals.

Life is full of adventure and trauma, love and sadness, joy and stress. It can be great or terrible. There will be ups and downs. But a lot of it depends on you and the choices you make. A life strategy will not only guide you but also build your resilience so that you're better able to recover from missteps.

Sophia, a doctor who suffered from a serious chronic illness, wrote to us after attending a workshop: "I realized I want to make more decisions, do really crazy things, enjoy small and big moments, celebrate successes, go to places I've never been, meet people I've never seen before, take breaks in between, follow my flow, and make myself my most important project in life!"

Now, go and do the same. Your life is your top strategic priority.

Originally published on hbr.org, December 5, 2023. Reprint H07XDL

COLLEEN AMMERMAN is the director of the Race, Gender & Equity Initiative at Harvard Business School and a coauthor, with Boris Groysberg, of *Glass Half-Broken* (Harvard Business Review Press, 2021).

ALLISON BAILEY is a senior partner and a managing director at Boston Consulting Group. She leads the firm's People & Organization practice globally and is a coauthor of several publications on the future of work, the bionic company, digital learning, and upskilling. She is also a fellow of the BCG Henderson Institute.

GOUTAM CHALLAGALLA is a professor of strategy and marketing at IMD.

RORY CHANNER is a founding partner at DCM Insights, a company that helps professional services firms improve business development, and was previously chief business development officer at McDermott Will & Emery.

FRÉDÉRIC DALSACE is a professor of marketing and strategy at IMD.

MATTHEW DIXON is a founding partner of DCM Insights. He is a co-author of *The Challenger Sale* and *The JOLT Effect*.

LEILA DOUMI is a PhD candidate in the Strategy Unit at Harvard Business School.

SUSANNE DYRCHS is an executive adviser, a coach, and a people strategy expert. She is also a BCG U faculty member and a coauthor of numerous publications on organizations, leadership, and talent. She has written a personal account of her transformational journey, *Wir-Zeit [Us Time]*, which was published in 2021.

KAREN FREEMAN is a partner at DCM Insights and was previously a senior manager of learning at McKinsey & Company.

SAGAR GOEL is a managing director and partner at Boston Consulting Group, Singapore, and a fellow at the BCG Henderson Institute.

BORIS GROYSBERG is a professor of business administration in the Organizational Behavior Unit at Harvard Business School and a faculty affiliate at the school's Race, Gender & Equity Initiative. He is a coauthor, with Colleen Ammerman, of *Glass Half-Broken* (Harvard Business Review Press, 2021).

ORSOLYA KOVÁCS-ONDREJKOVIC is an associate director at Boston Consulting Group, Zurich.

TED MCKENNA is a founding partner of DCM Insights and a coauthor of *The JOLT Effect*. He was previously a global knowledge leader at Russell Reynolds Associates.

LYNN S. PAINE is a Baker Foundation Professor and the John G. McLean Professor of Business Administration, Emerita, at Harvard Business School.

GARY P. PISANO is the Harry E. Figgie Jr. Professor of Business Administration at Harvard Business School and the author of *Creative Construction*.

HUGGY RAO is an organizational sociologist and the Atholl McBean Professor of Organizational Behavior at Stanford's Graduate School of Business. He is the author (with Robert I. Sutton) of *The Friction Project*.

LAURA MORGAN ROBERTS is a Frank M. Sands Sr. Associate Professor of Business Administration at the University of Virginia's Darden School of Business. She is an organizational psychologist and a coeditor of *Race, Work, and Leadership* (Harvard Business Review Press, 2019).

GINNI ROMETTY was the ninth chairman, president, and CEO of IBM. Today she serves on multiple boards and cochairs OneTen, a coalition committed to upskilling, hiring, and promoting one million Black Americans by 2030 into family-sustaining jobs and careers. She is the author of *Good Power* (Harvard Business Review Press, 2023).

RAFFAELLA SADUN is the Charles E. Wilson Professor of Business Administration at Harvard Business School.

WILLY C. SHIH is the Robert and Jane Cizik Professor of Management Practice at Harvard Business School.

RAINER STRACK is a senior partner emeritus and a senior adviser at Boston Consulting Group (BCG), where he built up and led the global People Strategy topic for 10 years. In 2014 he gave a widely watched TED Talk on the global workforce crisis. He formerly coheaded the Future of Work initiative for the World Economic Forum, and in 2021 he was inducted into *Personalmagazin*'s HR Hall of Fame. He is a fellow of the BCG Henderson Institute.

ROBERT I. SUTTON is an organizational psychologist and a professor of management science and engineering at Stanford University. He has written eight books, including (with Huggy Rao) *The Friction Project*.

JORGE TAMAYO is an assistant professor in the Strategy Unit at Harvard Business School.

JAMIL ZAKI is an associate professor of psychology at Stanford University, the director of its Social Neuroscience Lab, and the author of *The War for Kindness*. His latest book is *Hope for Cynics*.

Index

Engage with HBR content the way you want, on any device.

With HBR's subscription plans, you can access world-renowned case studies from Harvard Business School and receive four **free eBooks**. Download and customize prebuilt **slide decks and graphics** from our **Data & Visuals** collection. With HBR's archive, top 50 best-selling articles, and five new articles every day, HBR is more than just a magazine.

Subscribe Today
HBR.org/success

The most important management ideas all in one place.

We hope you enjoyed this book from *Harvard Business Review*. Now you can get even more with HBR's 10 Must Reads Boxed Set. From books on leadership and strategy to managing yourself and others, this 6-book collection delivers articles on the most essential business topics to help you succeed.

HBR's 10 Must Reads Series

The definitive collection of ideas and best practices on our most sought-after topics from the best minds in business.

- Change Management
- Collaboration
- Communication
- Emotional Intelligence
- Innovation
- Leadership
- Making Smart Decisions

- Managing Across Cultures
- Managing People
- Managing Yourself
- Strategic Marketing
- Strategy
- Teams
- The Essentials

hbr.org/mustreads

Buy for your team, clients, or event.
Visit hbr.org/bulksales for quantity discount rates.